T0277294

Cambridge Elements

Elements in Ethics
edited by
Ben Eggleston
University of Kansas
Dale E. Miller
Old Dominion University, Virginia

ETHICAL SUBJECTIVISM AND EXPRESSIVISM

Neil Sinclair
University of Nottingham

CAMBRIDGE
UNIVERSITY PRESS

CAMBRIDGE
UNIVERSITY PRESS

University Printing House, Cambridge CB2 8BS, United Kingdom

One Liberty Plaza, 20th Floor, New York, NY 10006, USA

477 Williamstown Road, Port Melbourne, VIC 3207, Australia

314–321, 3rd Floor, Plot 3, Splendor Forum, Jasola District Centre,
New Delhi – 110025, India

79 Anson Road, #06–04/06, Singapore 079906

Cambridge University Press is part of the University of Cambridge.

It furthers the University's mission by disseminating knowledge in the pursuit of
education, learning, and research at the highest international levels of excellence.

www.cambridge.org
Information on this title: www.cambridge.org/9781108706513
DOI: 10.1017/9781108581134

First published 2020

A catalogue record for this publication is available from the British Library.

ISBN 978-1-108-70651-3 Paperback
ISSN 2516-4031 (online)
ISSN 2516-4023 (print)

Ethical Subjectivism and Expressivism

Elements in Ethics

DOI: 10.1017/9781108581134
First published online: August 2020

Neil Sinclair
University of Nottingham
Author for correspondence: Neil Sinclair, neil.sinclair@nottingham.ac.uk

Abstract: Ethical subjectivists hold that moral judgements are descriptions of our attitudes. Expressivists hold that they are expressions of our attitudes. These views cook with the same ingredients – the natural world and our reactions to it – and have similar attractions. This Element assesses each of them by considering whether they can accommodate three central features of moral practice: the practicality of moral judgements, the phenomenon of moral disagreement, and the mind-independence of some moral truths. In the process, several different versions of subjectivism are distinguished (simple, communal, idealising, and normative) and key expressivist notions such as 'moral attitudes' and 'expression' are examined. Different meanings of 'subjective' and 'relative' are elucidated and it is considered whether subjectivism and expressivism make ethics 'subjective' or 'relative' in each of these senses.

Keywords: ethics, subjectivism, relativism, expressivism, moral disagreement

ISBNs: 9781108706513 (PB), 9781108581134 (OC)
ISSNs: 2516-4031 (online), 2516-4023 (print)

Contents

Introduction

This Element is written for the student who is new to these topics, though not to philosophy. It is an opinionated introduction to two influential theories of the nature of ethics. It aims to introduce these theories in ways that are sufficiently accessible to whet the appetite, yet sufficiently accurate so as not to mislead. To aid the reader, terms that first appear in **bold** feature in a glossary at the end of the Element.

1 Motivations and Methodology

1.1 Moral Debates

On 23 June 2016 the UK government asked 46,500,001 of its residents and citizens the following question:

> *Should the United Kingdom remain a member of the European Union or leave the European Union?*

Prior to the referendum, the Britain Stronger in Europe campaign argued for remaining, claiming that membership of the Union brought jobs, lower prices, and protections for workers' rights. The Vote Leave campaign argued for leaving on the basis that it would allow the UK to control its borders, make its own laws, and save £350 million per week.[1] Emotions ran high; accusations of dishonesty and treachery flew; opponents were branded 'disgraceful', 'shameful', 'abhorrent', even 'enemies of the people'. When the votes were counted, 17,410,742 people had voted to leave, 16,141,241 to remain. The consequences of this decision are still unfolding.

On 26 July 2017 the president of the United States announced that

> *the United States Government will not accept or allow Transgender individuals to serve in any capacity in the US Military.*

The president argued that the ban would allow the military to focus on 'decisive and overwhelming victory' and remove the burden of the 'tremendous medical costs and disruption that transgender in the military would entail'. The ban was strongly condemned by the American Civil Liberties Union, who called it 'outrageous' and 'desperate'. A *USA Today* editorial called it 'medically unethical', 'cruel', and 'senseless'. Others pointed out that the cost of transgender-related healthcare would amount to between 0.004 and 0.017 per cent of the

---

[1] See *The Brexit Collection: 2016 referendum* (LSE Digital Library) here: https://digital.library.lse
.ac.uk/collections/brexit/2016.

Defense Department's total healthcare spend. The debate about the permissible roles of transgender people in the US military continues.[2]

Each of these cases exemplifies a moral or ethical debate – an issue framed in terms of what we *should* do, what is *permissible*, what is *right* or *best*. From the large to the small scale, these issues pervade our lives. Our responses to them shape how we act individually and collectively. Such issues have three interesting features. First, they are intimately connected to motivation, action, and emotion. We want to know what we *should do*, or what the *right thing* to do is, because we want to know what *to* do – and our motivations and emotions affect what we *do* do. Second, they involve genuine moral disagreement. In each case there is a moral question at stake to which the disputing parties are attempting to find an answer. Finally, such issues are not settled by fiat. Merely thinking that leaving is the right thing to do does not make it so. The correct answers to moral questions are independent of our minds.

1.2 Metaethics and the Attractions of Subjectivism and Expressivism

Suppose you wanted not to *settle* these disputes but to understand the general class into which they fall. In other words, suppose you wanted to understand what a moral issue is and what is going on when people engage in moral debates. Then you would be what philosophers call a **metaethicist**. Subjectivism and expressivism are metaethical theories. In particular they are theories about what is going on when people make moral judgements such as the judgement that the UK should leave the European Union. According to **subjectivism** such judgements report attitudes, in something like the way that psychiatrists provide reports on the mental states of their patients. So to say that leaving is the right thing to do is to report on one's own positive feelings or emotions, or perhaps the feelings of one's tribe, class, or society. Ethics is a branch of psychology. According to **expressivism**, by contrast, moral judgements *express* attitudes, in something like the way that cheering expresses support of a football team. So to say that leaving is the right thing to do is to express a positive feeling or emotion towards leaving. Ethics is a branch of rhetoric, whose goal is to shape others' attitudes. (These characterisations are rough and will be refined as we progress.)

---

[2] CNN reported the President's comments on July 27 2017; see here: https://edition.cnn.com/2017/ 07/26/politics/trump-military-transgender/index.html. Events are the enemies of deadlines, and sometime after this Element was drafted, but before it was published, an even more significant event – the Covid-19 pandemic – highlighted multiple further examples of moral disputes, concerning, for example, the wisdom of various lockdown measures, how to ration scarce medical resources, and how to balance public health with economic prosperity. What I say in the text about moral debates applies just as well to these (as I write) startlingly salient problems.

The rest of this Element is concerned with the differences between, and plausibility of, these two theories; but before battle is joined, it is worth noting some shared features that make both attractive enough to investigate further.

First, subjectivism and expressivism cook with the same naturalistically respectable set of ingredients. According to both, all we need to cite in order to understand our moral practice is the natural world, our reactions to it, and the things we do with those reactions. Such elements are required anyway for any scientifically respectable account of human beings. Subjectivism and expressivism merely redeploy them to account for a very particular thing that human beings do to each other, namely moralise. This austere set of ingredients contrasts with the expansive set favoured by some (non-naturalist) moral realists, who hold that, as well as the properties countenanced by natural science, there exist irreducible moral properties such as goodness and rightness.[3] Ockham's razor famously asks us not to multiply entities beyond necessity; subjectivism and expressivism are more clean-shaven than most.

Second, this naturalistically kosher set of ingredients looks to be the correct set with which to explain the peculiar institution of morality. Both subjectivism and expressivism foreground our emotions, responses, attitudes, and motivations, and the thought that morality is concerned with such things is both intuitive and empirically grounded. Intuitive because we expect someone with moral stances to *care* in ways consistent with those stances. Empirically grounded because common experience and scientific studies show that moral judgements co-occur with, and are causally influenced by, emotions. One study, for instance (cited in Prinz 2006), found that people are more likely to make strong moral judgements after being primed to feel disgust (by being made to sit at a filthy desk).

A final appealing feature of subjectivism and expressivism is that the ingredients that they cook with are multiple, fecund, and permissive. The diversity of human emotional responses allows each theory to account for moralities with distinct emotional tones, such as sin-based moralities that foreground guilt, or paternalistic moralities that foreground pride and disappointment. Further, different emotions can be deployed to explain different types of moral verdict. For example, the difference between an action being merely bad and being shameful lies in the distinct emotion invoked by the latter. Finally, these ingredients are permissive insofar as they promise to explain other types of issues with which humans engage. For example, it is tempting to think that whether something is *beautiful*, *fashionable*, or *funny* can likewise be understood in terms of descriptions or expressions of attitudes. Subjectivism and

---

[3] Non-naturalist moral realists include Shafer-Landau (2003) and Enoch (2011).

expressivism are therefore worth studying not merely as theories of ethics but as adaptable models that can apply to other practices (especially areas where taking a realist view runs up against Ockham's razor).

So subjectivism and expressivism start as genuine contenders. In order to see whether this promise bears fruit we need to define our terms and consider our methodology. These are the tasks for sections 1.3 and 1.4.

1.3 Terminology and Initial Characterisations

Subjectivism and expressivism are primarily theories of moral judgements. By a **moral judgement** I mean the type of speech act performed when someone assertorically utters a moral sentence such as 'Murder is wrong'. So saying these words while performing a play or word-associating doesn't count; but reflecting on the issue of unlawful killing, coming to consider that it is not permissible, and then voicing that thought by saying 'Murder is wrong', does count.

What about the thought thus voiced or expressed? What is involved in *thinking* that murder is wrong? I call this a **moral commitment**. It is a mental state, and its nature is one of the points at issue between subjectivists and expressivists. Commitments are more enduring than judgements: I can think that murder is wrong long before I voice this opinion. Commitments are mental states that people *have* or *are in*, whereas judgements are acts of speech that people *make* or *perform*. Nevertheless the connections between them are close – a standard assumption is that judgements express commitments.[4]

Subjectivism and expressivism both talk about attitudes, so this term also needs elucidation. By an **attitude** I mean a mental state that provides us with a goal and some motivation to pursue it. This is in contrast with cognitions, which provide us with a depiction of the way the world is that is independent of any direction as to what to do about it. Desires are attitudes, insofar as my desire for chocolate, say, provides me with a goal (to have chocolate) and some motivation to act in ways that I believe will help me secure that goal. This motivation need not be conclusive – I may have a stronger desire to lose weight, for example – but it is real, nonetheless. In contrast my belief that the Netherlands is flat is a cognition insofar as it represents the lay of the land but gives me no guidance as to what to do about that fact. How I end up acting will largely depend on a complex interplay between my attitudes and cognitions. If I desire chocolate and believe there to be some in the fridge, then, other things

---

[4] Some use the term 'moral utterance' to refer to the speech act I call a moral judgement and 'moral judgement' to refer to the mental state I am calling a moral commitment. Like most metaethical terminology, usage is treacherous, but the important distinction to remember is that between the speech act and the mental state.

being equal, I will go to the fridge. Things are seldom equal, of course, since opposed attitudes may result in me channelling my efforts in other directions. In every case, however, action seems to require both a goal-setting attitude and a cognition that provides the agent with an idea of how to pursue that goal.

Desires are one kind of attitude, but there are others. Emotions, preferences, intentions, aversions, phobias, approvals, and disapprovals all fall into this category insofar as they provide motivational direction. Conversely, perceptions and intuitions seem to be cognitions insofar as they depict the world. The attitude/cognition distinction has a venerable history, being traceable from Plato, through David Hume, to modern philosophers such as Elizabeth Anscombe and David Lewis.[5]

The final terms in need of definition are **report** and **express**. According to subjectivism moral judgements report attitudes; according to expressivism they express attitudes. So what is the difference? Roughly, when we report attitudes, we describe them. To describe is to represent the world as being a certain way or to make a claim about the way things are. So when we report *attitudes*, we make a claim about the ways things are *psychologically*, and when we report our *own* attitudes, we make a claim about the way things are with *our own* psychology. Descriptions can be accurate or inaccurate, true or false. By contrast when we express attitudes, we do something other than report them. We voice them, externalise them, lay them out before others. These metaphors get us somewhere, but they remain mysterious (and potentially misleading) – we shall have to return to this issue later (see Section 5.2.2). For now, it is worth noting some structural features of expression. First, when we express attitudes, we do not report or describe. Thus when we express attitudes there is no possibility of that expression being 'accurate' or 'inaccurate' – or at least no sense of it being accurate or inaccurate *as a description*. Likewise, there is no possibility of it being true or false, agreed or disagreed with – or at least, no sense in it being these things *qua description*. (Whether there are other senses in which expressions of attitudes can be these things is discussed in Section 5.2.3.) Second, it is commonly assumed that whatever it means to say that moral judgements express attitudes, regular non-moral judgements – such as my judgement that grass is green – express beliefs in just the same way.[6] The thought here is that to describe is to express a belief, and regular non-moral judgements function to describe.

These assumptions suggest improved definitions of expressivism and subjectivism. According to expressivism moral judgements express our attitudes;

---

[5] See Plato's *Republic*, Hume's *A Treatise of Human Nature* (book 2), Anscombe (1957), and Lewis (1988).

[6] See, for example, Gibbard (2003: 75) and Schroeder (2008: 18).

and remembering that moral commitments just are the mental states expressed by moral judgements, we can characterise expressivism as:

> E. Moral judgements express attitudes. Hence moral commitments are attitudes.

According to subjectivism moral judgements report or describe attitudes. To describe is to express a belief, so moral judgements express beliefs about attitudes. Thus:

> S. Moral judgements express beliefs about attitudes (i.e. they describe attitudes). Hence moral commitments are beliefs about attitudes.

As we shall see, these characterisations are still deficient but they highlight the fact that one point of contention between expressivism and subjectivism concerns the nature of moral commitments: are they attitudes or beliefs about attitudes?

1.4 Methodology

1.4.1 Moral Practice, Semantics, and Metasemantics

Subjectivism and expressivism are theories of moral judgement, but much else besides. Moral judgements are one small part of the phenomenon of **moral practice**, which includes the myriad ways in which moral concepts feature in human thought, language, and interaction. Other parts of this practice include moral phenomenology (what it is like to intuit a moral fact), moral deliberation (the thought processes that lead to forming or revising one's moral views), moral debate (the public exchange of moral views), moral argument (inferring moral claims from others), and moral guidance (having one's feelings and actions shaped by moral thought and debate). Any subjectivist or expressivist worth their salt will have something to say about all these things. Nevertheless I shall follow tradition and focus primarily on moral judgements. This is justifiable both insofar as it makes the issues tractable and because in most cases the account of the other aspects of moral practice is strongly suggested by the account of moral judgements.

Even with this narrower focus, however, we need to consider what it means to be a *theory* of moral judgements. Subjectivism and expressivism are standardly taken to be theories that *give* or *explain* the *meaning* of these judgements. So when expressivists claim that moral judgements express attitudes, they are not claiming that this is a contingent or accidental feature of their usage. They are claiming that the fact that moral judgements express attitudes is a necessary part of the explanation of their meaning.

In this sense subjectivism and expressivism are *semantic* theories, concerned with *meaning*. Yet we need to be careful here, because the terminology of 'semantics' risks ambiguity. For by 'semantic theory' we can mean either **first-order semantic theory** or **metasemantic theory**. I think that subjectivism and expressivism are best understood as the latter, but to explain why we first need to understand the distinction.

Suppose you are a monolingual English speaker interested in the meaning of the judgement 'Schnee ist weiß'. I tell you that 'Schnee ist weiß' is German and means that snow is white. It seems there has been some progress. I have given you a first-order semantic theory for this judgement: a theory that tells you what it means, that *gives* you its meaning.

Suppose on the other hand that you are a bilingual English and German speaker who knows full well what 'Schnee ist weiß' means. Yet still, you want to know *why* this type of judgement, as typically made by actual speakers of German, means what it does. Why is it that just these words allow speakers of German to make just this claim about just these things? After all there is nothing necessary about the fact that 'Schnee' refers to snow – the same string of letters could have easily referred to snowshoes, or pyramids. One tempting answer is that the judgement has the stable (that is, non-context-specific) meaning it does in virtue of characteristically expressing or propounding a particular belief, viz. the belief that snow is white. This is not a complete theory of meaning, to be sure – it explains the *meaning* of a type of judgement in terms of a suspiciously similar notion of the *content* of a belief characteristically expressed – but it is a substantive theory, nonetheless.[7] It is a *metasemantic* theory insofar as it provides an account of the contingent facts that explain why a particular type of judgement, as typically made by a group of people, has the stable meaning that it does.

There is a distinction, then, between theories that *give* you the meaning of a type of judgement and theories that *explain* why that judgement has the meaning it does. I take subjectivism and expressivism to be theories of the latter sort.[8] Subjectivists claim that we can explain the meaning of moral judgements in terms of their characteristic ability to express beliefs about attitudes. Expressivists claim that we can explain the meaning of moral judgements in terms of their characteristic ability to express attitudes. If we define the **semantic function** of a set of judgements as the characteristic function that

---

[7] This is sometimes called 'ideationism' or a 'psychologising' or 'dog-legged' approach to meaning. See Blackburn (1984: 39–45), Laurence (1996), and Ridge (2014: 107).

[8] For the recently popular idea that key issues in metaethics are metasemantic rather than semantic, see, for example, Chrisman (2012) and Ridge (2014).

explains their stable meaning, then we can further refine our two theories as follows:

> S*. The semantic function of moral judgements is to express beliefs about attitudes (i.e. to describe those attitudes). Hence moral commitments are beliefs about attitudes.

> E*. The semantic function of moral judgements is to express attitudes. Hence moral commitments are attitudes.

Unfortunately, the existing literature on subjectivism and expressivism often misses the distinction between first-order semantics and metasemantics. It is common, for example, to take expressivism to be a semantic theory that *gives* meanings or paraphrases of moral judgements.[9] This is a mistake. Expressivism is no more a theory that gives you meanings than Marxism is a theory that gives you capital. Both theories explain their targets rather than producing them.

There are many reasons why the distinction between first-order semantics and metasemantics is overlooked, but one salient from the current context is that S* is a metasemantic theory that quickly generates claims in first-order semantics as well. According to S* the meaning of moral judgements is explained in terms of those judgements expressing beliefs about attitudes. Further, it seems a plausible independent assumption that, where the semantic function of a judgement is to express a belief, the meaning of that judgement is the same as the content of the belief expressed.[10] It follows that, according to S*, the meaning of moral judgements is given by claims about attitudes. Thus S* quickly generates first-order semantic claims (or 'analyses') of the sort:

> S1. 'Murder is wrong' means 'I disapprove of murder'.

Nevertheless the metasemantic claim S* remains distinct from the first-order semantic claim S1. The tendency, when discussing subjectivism, to focus the latter, and then to consider expressivism a *rival* to subjectivism, is one source of the mistaken thought that expressivism, too, provides psychological paraphrases of moral judgements.

1.4.2 First Desideratum: Accommodation

So subjectivism and expressivism are metasemantic theories, that is, theories of those facts in virtue of which moral judgements have the meaning that they do.

---

[9] For example, Cuneo (2006: 35), Olson (2010), and Wright (1992: 11).
[10] See Schroeder (2008): 32–3.

In a more expansive sense they are also theories of the moral practice that grows up with and surrounds such judgements. Yet how are such theories to be judged? Like many metaethicists, I accept two desiderata for metaethical theories.[11] The first is accommodation. A good metaethical theory should be able to **accommodate** the forms of ordinary moral practice and the assumptions of those who engage with it. To accommodate a form or assumption is to provide an explanation of why a practice with that form or assumption has arisen and (ideally) to justify that practice carrying on with that form or assumption (to accommodate is to learn to live with, to cohabit).[12] The forms of moral practice include the fact that moral judgements often come to us unbidden, the fact that moral judgements are made using sentences of indicative form, the fact that moral judgements feature in public debates, and the fact that people offer reasons in support of moral claims. Furthermore, people who engage in moral practice make assumptions when doing so. For example, they assume that some actions are wrong, others right, that there is such a thing as moral disagreement, that debate can help discover answers to moral questions, that merely making a moral judgement does not make it correct, and so on. These assumptions are revealed in people's behaviour as much as their explicit beliefs.

I shall refer to these forms and assumptions as the 'features' of moral practice. The reason that a good metaethical theory needs to accommodate them is that, if it did not, it would fail to be a theory of *moral* practice at all. For example, a metaethical theory that could not explain why moral sentences have indicative form and predicts instead that they have imperative form (like 'Shut the door!') seems to be a theory of something other than our actual practice.

There are hundreds of features of moral practice that good metaethical theories should accommodate. To make things tractable, I will consider just three. These are the practicality of moral judgements, moral disagreement, and moral mind-independence. The next three subsections say a little about each. The rest of this Element will then consider whether various versions of subjectivism and expressivism can accommodate them. Of course, the result will not be exhaustive. For each feature of moral practice that is not discussed there will be a dimension of the evaluation of these theories that is missing. So my approach is necessarily partial; but I hope that by focusing tightly on three features this

---

[11] A canonical statement is Timmons (1999: 12).

[12] Note that there are two senses of 'accommodation' in play here: a weaker sense that demands only *explanation* and a stronger sense that also demands *justification* or *vindication* of the relevant form or assumption. The argument I give in the next paragraph seems only to support the former, and there is genuine controversy about the latter: see Section 1.4.4, Loeb (2007), and Sinclair (2012).

Element will provide the reader with an indication of the sort of accommodation strategies subjectivists and expressivists can deploy, as well as the characteristic problems with those strategies – thus equipping the reader with the tools to complete a more thorough assessment of both views.

1.4.2.1 Practicality

Consider first the fact that moral judgements are practical. There are at least two parts to this. First, moral judgements answer practical questions. Return to the issue of the UK's relationship with the European Union, as set out in the 2016 referendum question. What are we to do: leave or remain? This is a practical question, seemingly answered by the claim that the *right* thing to do, the thing we *should* do, is leave (or remain). Moral judgements seem to have just the right sort of meaning – **normative meaning** – to help us answer such practical questions. By contrast, many non-moral judgements lack such content. Suppose I was told that leaving will lead to higher prices. That wouldn't settle the issue of what to do, since I may not care about higher prices.[13]

The second dimension of practicality concerns the connection to motivation. There seems to be a necessary connection between making a (sincere) moral judgement and being appropriately motivated by it. The necessity of this connection is revealed by the fact that, when faced with an agent who (apparently sincerely) judged that leaving was the right thing to do and yet who showed no indication of supporting the leave campaign, no indication of regretting the fact they felt no such motivation, and even voted remain, then we would begin to doubt that they understood what it means to call an action 'right'. It is important to note that the necessary connection here is between moral judgement and appropriate *motivation*, not moral judgement and appropriate *action*. A motivation is an attitude – an internal push to action – but how I end up acting depends on how all my motivations interact, and some motivations may be overridden by others. It would be an absurdly strong thesis to say that there is a necessary connection between moral judgement and appropriate *action*, for this would entail that people always act in accord with their moral judgements, as if people always lived up to their moral ideals. Note also that even the connection between moral judgement and *motivation* is not without exception. We are comfortable with the thought that the connection can break down in exceptional cases, for example in corrupted sadists (who are now explicitly motivated away from good and towards evil), jaded politicians (who have been on the political scene for too long, and seen too much, to remain moved by their ideological beliefs), or motivationally drained parents

---

[13] This paragraph summarises ideas from Blackburn (1998: 70, 90–1).

(who are simply too tired to feel any motivation to act as they think they ought). We recognise too, however, that such cases are not normal and require some sort of background story to be comprehensible. The best we can say, therefore, is that, necessarily, if an agent makes a moral judgement, then, in normal circumstances, she will possess an appropriate motivation. This is sometimes called **motivational internalism**.[14]

What is the connection between the two senses of practicality – normative meaning and motivational internalism? A set of judgements cannot be practical in the former sense unless they are practical in the latter. This is because a practical question has not been answered – practical deliberation has not ended – until the agent acts or forms an intention to act, and having a motivation is a necessary precursor to action and intention. On the other hand, a set of judgements *could* be practical in the sense of being tightly connected to motivation, without having normative meaning. Suppose, for example, that I am a compulsive gambler, so that whenever I hear that a venue has slot machines I am compelled to go there. Then there is a psychologically necessary connection between my judgement that 'The venue has slot machines' and being motivated to go; but though my judgement thereby *forecloses* the question of whether to go (it makes it moot), it does not *answer* that question. A connection to motivation needs to be of the correct sort in order for a judgement to properly answer a practical question (rather than merely foreclose it), and the 'correct sort' seems to be the sort provided by the fact that moral judgements (unlike my judgement about slot machines) have normative meaning.[15]

The interesting feature of moral judgements, therefore, is not just that they are necessarily connected to motivation but that they have a particular sort of meaning – that is, normative meaning – and in part because of that are necessarily connected to motivation.

1.4.2.2 Disagreement

Consider, next, moral disagreement. It is an interesting fact about moral judgements that they are capable of being disagreed with. Return to the UK referendum. Leavers disagreed with Remainers, and this, it seems, was a moral dispute insofar as it concerned what the UK *should* do. Such disagreements have several interesting aspects. First, they are *genuine* disagreements, insofar as they involve a shared subject matter about which the two sides are in dispute. In

---

[14] For exposition of the exceptional cases see Stocker (1979), Dreier (1990), and Blackburn (1998: ch. 3). A helpful taxonomy of the varieties of 'internalism' is van Roojen (2015): 54–9.
[15] See also Smith (1989: 92–3).

this they contrast with merely apparent disagreements. For example, before my children got to grips with the proper meaning of the word 'I', they would have 'disagreements' of the following sort. The eldest says, 'I'm four years old'. The youngest says, 'No! I'm two'. The eldest replies, louder this time, 'No! I am four'. The youngest, now very irate, 'Two!' Tantrums ensue. This disagreement is merely apparent, since there is no shared subject matter, no single referent of 'I'. The disagreement between Leavers and Remainers, by contrast, was genuine. It was more than words uttered confrontationally.

A second aspect of moral disagreements is that they are distinctively *moral*. That is to say that they are disagreements that are *captured* by moral judgements. This contrasts with cases where disagreement accompanies a set of judgements but is not focused on them. Suppose that Abe says, 'I only like chilli' and Betty says, 'I don't like chilli'. In one sense, they disagree: they have conflicting tastes that will make choosing a date venue tricky. Yet this disagreement is not about what each of them *likes* – both of them may have full knowledge of each other's preferences; and since their judgements *are* about what they like, it follows that their judgements do not capture their disagreement. We might say that the disagreement *attends* the judgements, without being *captured* by them. The case of the EU referendum is different: not only did Leavers and Remainers disagree *by* making moral judgements, they disagreed *in* moral judgement – they disagreed precisely over whether leaving the EU was the *right* thing to do.

A final feature of moral disagreement is that it is its own thing or *sui generis*.[16] Moral disagreement can persist even when complete agreement has been reached on relevant non-moral matters. For example, some Leavers and Remainers may have agreed about all the non-moral features of leaving the European Union (the likely effects on prices, immigration, taxes, and so on) and yet still disagreed about whether the UK should leave. Not all moral disputes are like this, of course, since some of them are resolved once the non-moral facts are agreed, but each moral dispute has the potential to outrun the non-moral facts in this way, and in just this sense moral disagreement is *sui generis*. (Perhaps aesthetic disagreements are *sui generis* in a similar way.)

So moral judgements are the sorts of things that can be disagreed with, and the resulting disagreement is genuine, moral, and *sui generis*. It is an interesting fact about moral issues that they permit disagreement of this kind, and any metaethical theory needs to accommodate it.

---

[16] See Stevenson (1948).

1.4.2.3 Mind-Independence

Murder is wrong. It is not wrong, however, because I think it is; and it is not wrong because I don't like it or because it disgusts me. Nor is it wrong because *most* people think it is, dislike it, or are disgusted by it. Rather murder is wrong because of its own features, such as its unfortunate tendency to end lives; and what goes for the wrongness of murder goes for many other moral facts. In general, the moral facts about a thing do not depend on our thoughts about, or our attitudes towards, that thing. Moral facts are mind-independent in just this sense. If they were not, then moral practice would be very different from how it actually is: the moral facts would change as people's attitudes change and we would investigate them by investigating people's attitudes. Yet, though people's *moral commitments* frequently change (and improve), moral facts generally do not. Some eighteenth-century merchants believed that slavery was morally permissible, whereas we believe it is wrong; but the moral fact has not changed. Slavery was wrong in the eighteenth century (though some at the time mistakenly thought otherwise). Moreover it was wrong then (as now) not because of our attitudes towards it but because of the terrible suffering and indignities it involved.

At any rate, the thought that moral facts are mind-independent in this way seems to be an assumption of those who make moral judgements – an assumption that needs accommodating. Hence a metaethical theory should be able to explain why people typically assume that moral facts are mind-independent, and (ideally) why doing so is legitimate.

Our task, then, is to consider how subjectivism and expressivism fare in accommodating these features of moral practice. Can each theory explain the practicality of moral judgements, give an account of moral disagreement, and vindicate the assumption that moral facts are mind-independent? Answering these questions will not decisively settle the debate between subjectivism and expressivism, since there are many more features of moral practice that we could consider. It will, however, give us some indication of their strengths and weaknesses, laying the ground for a more complete assessment.

1.4.3 Second Desideratum: Consilience

How should we judge competing accommodation projects? Of course, they must be judged on whether they really do accommodate the features in question, but are there other constraints? This brings us to the second desideratum for metaethical theories: *consilience*. This is the thought that, in accommodating the features of moral practice, a good metaethical theory should cohere with our wider philosophical theories. For example, a metaethical theory is plausible to the extent that what it says about *moral* meaning coheres with a plausible *general* theory of meaning; to the extent that what it says about *moral* facts coheres with a plausible *general* theory of facts; to the extent that what it says about moral *knowledge* coheres with a plausible *general* theory of knowledge; and so on. Consilience captures the thought that a good metaethical theory should fit the moral sphere into our wider understanding of the world and the place of humans within it.

So what is this wider understanding? For many philosophers – including virtually all who identify as subjectivists and expressivists – it is a naturalistic understanding. To understand the world naturalistically is to understand it through the methods and materials of the natural sciences, such as psychology, biology, and physics. On this view the task for metaethics is to accommodate the features of moral practice while simultaneously understanding human beings solely in natural terms, as 'frail complexes of perishable tissue' (Blackburn 1998: 48). A theory that (for example) postulated a unique realm of moral properties, entirely distinct from anything countenanced in natural science, would fail in this regard.

It is not necessary to understand consilience in terms of natural science.[17] The general point is just that one's understanding of moral practice should cohere with one's wider views of the sorts of facts and processes the world contains. It is controversial whether naturalism is the most plausible 'wider view' – but if it is then this plays in favour of subjectivism and expressivism, since they use only naturalistically respectable materials to accommodate the features of moral practice.

1.4.4 Revisionism

So metaethical theories should be judged insofar as they accommodate the features of moral practice, in a way that coheres with our best wider theories of human beings and the world in which they live. There are reasons, however, to think that no theory will be wholly successful in this task. First, because it is unlikely that all the features of actual moral practice are manifestations of a single unified practice, that has a unified goal, in light of which all of its features make sense. Second, because it is likely that false metaethical theories have themselves infected the practice, so that some reflective participants (philosophers, perhaps) engage in the practice with a false understanding of their activities built in. In other words, actual moral practice is most likely too messy, plural, and theory-saturated to warrant a single accommodation-story. Most metaethical

---

[17] For a defence of naturalism see Papineau (1993).

theories, therefore, are *revisionary* to a certain extent. They propose that certain features of moral practice cannot be accommodated and should be abandoned (perhaps to be replaced by less problematic surrogates). A theory may claim, for instance, that (some aspects of) the practicality of moral judgements, or moral disagreement, simply cannot be accommodated and should be abandoned.

How should we judge between competing revisionary theories? Each feature of moral practice that a theory revises carries an explanatory cost, but this cost can be met so long as the resulting theory can show how all the important things that human beings say and do using moral practice, and all the substantive debates that practice involves, are preserved under the recommended revised practice. For example, it will be no good recommending that we replace moral practice with a system of communal chanting, if by doing so we lose an important aspect of the way we interact with each other and the world. What these important aspects are is, of course, a metaethical issue. Thus in order to be plausible a revisionary metaethical theory must first defend an account of the way that moral practice helps us relate in worthwhile ways to the world and to each other, and then show how, given this account, most (if not all) of the features of that practice are to be expected.

1.5 Looking Ahead

In what follows I consider whether subjectivism and expressivism can accommodate practicality, disagreement, and mind-independence. I shall say little about consilience, since I will assume that, in most forms, subjectivism and expressivism are compatible with a naturalistic world view. I will suggest, however, that neither theory is wholly successful in accommodating these features – both are partly revisionary. It is important to remember, therefore, that being revisionary is not fatal to a metaethical theory. Whenever a theory demands revision, we must ask whether the aspect of our practice it asks us to revise is peripheral enough not to be missed, or so central that abandoning it changes our practice beyond reasonable recognition. If any of the revisions required by subjectivism and expressivism are considered radical in this way, then one may wish to consider the other metaethical theories explored in this series.

2 'Subjective' and 'Relative'

One often hears the claim that ethics is subjective or relative, but what does this mean exactly? Different people will intend different things by these words. Our first task is to sort out these ambiguities, so that we can properly assesses

subjectivism and expressivism. That, at any rate, is the aim of Section 2 of this
Element.

2.1 Provisional Characterisations

Is ethics subjective? That depends on what you mean by 'subjective' – and also
by 'ethics'. Since there are many things you might mean by either, it is unhelpful
to define 'subjectivism' as the view that ethics is subjective. Instead, in Section
1.4.1 I defined subjectivism, provisionally, thus:

> S*. The semantic function of moral judgements is to express beliefs about
> attitudes. Hence moral commitments are beliefs about attitudes.

I also accepted the assumption that, where the semantic function of a judgement
is to express a belief, the meaning of that judgement is the same as the content of
the belief. So, for example, according to the version of S* that claims that
a person's moral judgements express beliefs about *their own* attitudes, something like the following will also be true:

> S1. 'Murder is wrong' means 'I disapprove of murder'.

By contrast, I defined expressivism as the view that:

> E*. The semantic function of moral judgements is to express attitudes. Hence
> moral commitments are attitudes.

No claim analogous to S1 follows from E*, since the assumption that took us
from S* to S1 refers only to judgements that express beliefs, not judgements that
express attitudes.

With these theories in mind, we can ask more precise questions: Is ethics
subjective *according to each of these views*? Is it relative? Unfortunately these
are still not great questions to ask, since the terms 'subjective' and 'relative'
remain undefined. In the next two subsections I explore some possible definitions and consider whether, according to each, subjectivism and expressivism
make ethics subjective or relative.

2.2 'Subjective'

Here are some of the things we might mean by 'subjective'.[18] First:

> (i) A phenomenon is subjective to the extent that it can be explained in terms
> of psychological states.

---

[18] The senses of 'subjective' distinguished here are influenced by the discussion in Kirchin (2012:
26–30).

Witch trials, mass hysteria, and referenda results are subjective in this sense, whereas volcanic eruptions and planetary motions are not. According to both subjectivism and expressivism our moral judgements in particular, and our moral practices more generally, are subjective in sense (i). On both views, moral practice is essentially something that humans do to each other – something that can be explained in terms of humans and their attitudes. In particular both views hold that we do not need to refer to an extra realm of moral facts or properties in order to explain the meaning of moral judgements.

Here is another sense of 'subjective':

> (ii) A judgement or property is subjective to the extent that it can be *analysed* in terms of psychological states.

The judgements that sulphur is nauseating and that metaphysics is tiresome are subjective in this sense. The former means that exposure to sulphur causes nausea; the latter that exposure to metaphysics causes tiredness. These are *analyses* of *judgements*: they tell us what they mean or decompose their meaning into simpler parts. They are subjective insofar as they tell us that what those judgements mean is something about psychological states. In a closely related sense, a *property* can be analysed by being broken down into *its* constituent parts. (A judgement is a linguistic act with meaning, whereas a property is a quality that, when instantiated, is a part of a fact. For example, if I judge that my desk is white, I am ascribing the property of whiteness to my desk. If my judgement is correct, there really is a fact out there in the world – *the whiteness of my desk* – that is partly made up of an instance of the property of whiteness. For more on property analysis, see Schroeder 2007: ch. 4.) For an example of this property analysis, consider the property of being nauseating. This can be analysed in terms of the properties of *being a cause* and *feeling sick*: the property of being nauseating just is the property of being such as to *cause* people to *feel sick*. Insofar as this property analysis mentions a psychological state, the property thus analysed is *subjective* in sense (ii). Note that in both types of case an analysis need not be obvious or transparent. It can take some investigation to discover the meaning of judgements or the structure of properties. Yet where those meanings or structures are given by psychological states, the analysis is subjective in sense (ii).

According to subjectivism moral judgements or properties can be analysed in terms of psychological states. On one version of subjectivism, for instance, to judge that murder is wrong is to judge that one disapproves of it. Hence the property of being wrong just is the property of being disapproved of. According to expressivism, by contrast, moral judgements cannot be analysed in psychological terms, since to analyse a judgement is to give a different judgement equivalent in meaning, and no psychological judgement has the same expressive type of meaning as moral judgements – psychological judgements describe rather than express attitudes.[19] Furthermore, according to expressivism, there are no moral properties, so these too cannot be analysed in psychological terms (see Section 5.2.3). Hence in sense (ii) subjectivism makes ethics subjective, but expressivism does not.

Consider next:

> (iii) A judgement is subjective if it cannot be incorrect.

In the most relevant sense, a judgement is incapable of being incorrect insofar as the notions of correctness and incorrectness are simply out of place for judgements of its type. The judgements that chilli is tasty and that the Packers are awesome are perhaps like this: there are simply no standards of correctness or incorrectness that apply to them, and in that sense they are subjective.

When it comes to moral judgements, subjectivism does *not* make moral judgements subjective in sense (iii). According to subjectivism moral judgements are judgements made correct by the psychology of some actual or possible people. Such judgements can therefore be incorrect. For example, I may judge that the majority of my neighbours approve of my loud parties when in fact they do not. I may even be incorrect about my own psychological states, for example if I judge that I like doughnuts when what I really like is the music they play in the doughnut shop.

The issue of whether, if expressivism is true, moral judgements are subjective in sense (iii) is somewhat harder. Certainly, some early expressivists held that moral judgements cannot be correct or incorrect. However, later expressivists have tried to resist this conclusion, arguing that it can make sense, if expressivism is true, to say that some moral judgements are correct and others incorrect. The details of this argument await in Section 5.2.3. For now, note that, accepting it, it follows that early versions of expressivism do, whereas later versions do not, make ethics subjective in sense (iii).

Consider next:

> (iv) A judgement is subjective to the extent that whether it is correct necessarily depends on psychological states (i.e. its correctness conditions are psychological).

For example, whether the judgement that Brian is awake is correct necessarily depends on Brian's psychological states; and whether the judgement that 'The Big One' rollercoaster is scary is correct depends on the psychological states of

---

[19] See Blackburn (1998: 50) and Gibbard (2003: 6).

the people who ride it. By contrast, whether the judgement that Etna is erupting is correct does not necessarily depend on anyone's actual or possible psychological states. This type of subjectivity is closely connected to the second: if a judgement is *analysed* in terms of psychological states, then whether it is correct depends on those same states. Similarly, if a *property* is analysed in terms of psychological properties, then whether a judgement ascribing that property is correct will depend on those properties. Since subjectivism makes moral judgements subjective in the second sense, it also makes them subjective in sense (iv).

Early expressivists deny that moral judgements have correctness conditions, so they must deny that those correctness conditions are psychological. A more interesting question is whether this fourth sense of subjectivity applies to later versions of expressivism. That depends on just how these versions make sense of the thought that moral judgements can be correct or incorrect. Certainly many opponents have thought that later expressivists, like subjectivists, must accept that the correctness of moral judgements necessarily depends on psychology. Whether this accusation can be made to stick is discussed in Section 5.2.3.

Table 1 summarises the discussion so far.

No doubt there are other things we may mean by calling a judgement 'subjective' (sometimes, for example, we mean that it is biased, introspective,

Table 1 Is ethics subjective, according to subjectivism and expressivism?

Senses of 'subjective'→	(i) Can moral practice be explained in terms of psychology (and not irreducible moral properties)?	(ii) Can moral judgements or properies be analysed in terms of psychology?	(iii) Are moral judgements such that they cannot be incorrect?	(iv) Does the correctness of moral judgements necessarily depend on psychology?
Subjectivism	YES	YES	NO	YES
Early Expressivism (e.g. Ayer)	YES	NO	YES	NO
Later Expressivism (e.g. Blackburn)	YES	NO	NO	?

or only graspable by beings like us); but in order to move the discussion along, we need to consider a closely related issue: **relativism**.

2.3 'Relative'

Is ethics relative, according to subjectivism and expressivism? Again, this depends on what one means by 'ethics' and by 'relative'. Section 2.2 provides some clarity on the former: by 'ethics' we could mean moral practice in general, the moral judgements we make, the correctness conditions of those judgements, or the moral properties ascribed by such judgements. So what about 'relative'?

In a standard sense, a judgement is **relative** when whether it is correct depends on one among a number of possible frames of reference or contexts and *absolute* when it does not so depend (see Dreier 1990: 7). For example, the judgement 'I am male' is relative because whether or not it is correct depends on the context of who is making it: those very same words, said by someone else, would be incorrect. Likewise the judgement 'Bob is moving' is relative because whether or not it is correct depends on our frame of reference when we assess it. Bob may be stationary with respect to the fellow passengers in his train compartment but moving very quickly with respect to the crowd on the platform. There are therefore two ways in which a judgement might be relative: either because the claim made by the judgement (i.e. in uttering the same words) varies in different contexts of use (as in the case of 'I am male') or because the claim made by the judgement is the same in all contexts of use, but whether or not that claim is correct depends on the context of assessment (as in the case of 'Bob is moving').[20]

So are moral judgements relative, according to subjectivism? The slightly annoying answer to this question is that it has no single answer. On some versions of subjectivism moral judgements are relative, on others they are not. This is because, at the general level, all subjectivism says is that moral judgements are judgements about psychology (or judgements made true by facts about psychology) and some judgements (and facts) about psychology are relative and some are not. For example, 'I approve of this' is a psychological judgement that is relative, since whether or not it is true depends on the particular context of who is making it. By contrast 'Bob is sentient' is a psychological judgement that is not relative, since whether it is true depends on a single context and point of evaluation, namely Bob. Thus, as we shall see, there is scope for versions of subjectivism that are relativist and versions that are absolute. There is even scope for versions that sit somewhere in between. According to Lewis's conditional relativism, for example, it is unclear how many possible frames of reference for moral judgements there are, but we

---

[20] For these two types of relativism see Stojanovic (2018).

proceed on the basis that there are fewer, until we explicitly discover otherwise (see Section 4.2.1). This is like ordering steak for the whole table, hoping that no vegetarians show up.

What about expressivism? Are moral judgements relative, according to expressivism? Again the issue is unclear. According to the first type of relativism judgements are relative insofar as their *content* (the claims they make) varies according to their context of use; but it is unclear what expressivism says about the content of moral judgements (remember, expressivists deny that they are offering *analyses*). According to the second type of relativism judgements are relative insofar as their correctness conditions vary according to the context of assessment; but again it is unclear what expressivists say about the correctness conditions of moral judgements. These issues will have to wait until Section 5.

It is worth noting that there is at least one sense in which subjectivists and expressivists accept that ethics is relative. This is the sense in which different people make different moral judgements and have different moral commitments. This diversity of moral opinion is hard to deny and can no doubt be explained by citing features of people's contexts that influence the moral positions they take. Yet to claim that people in different contexts make different moral judgements is not to claim that the correctness of those judgements is solely determined by those contexts. Relativism in the former sense (sometimes called 'descriptive relativism') is uncontroversial. In the latter sense (sometimes called 'metaethical relativism') it is hugely controversial.

3 Simple Subjectivism

This chapter assesses several versions of subjectivism. In particular it considers whether each can accommodate the features of moral practice set out in Section 1.4.2: the practicality of moral judgements, moral disagreement, and moral mind-independence.

3.1 Hobbes

Consider first *simple subjectivism*, some early statements of which come from Thomas Hobbes's *Leviathan*:

> For these words of Good, evill, and Contemptible, are ever used with relation to the person that useth them: There being nothing simply and absolutely so; nor any common Rule of Good and evill, to be taken from the nature of the objects themselves; but from the Person of the man (where there is no Commonwealth;) or, (in a Common-wealth,) from the Person that representeth it . . .[21]

---

[21] Chapter 6.

> Morall Philosophy is nothing else but the Science of what is Good, and Evill,
> in the conversation, and Society of mankind. Good, and Evill, are names that
> signifie our Appetites, and Aversions; which in different tempers, customes,
> and doctrines of men, are different . . .[22]

One way of understanding these passages is as offering the following biconditional:

SS. X is (morally) good if and only if X is approved of by the speaker.[23]

On this view when I judge that 'X is good' my judgement will be correct just in case it accurately represents my approval of X, that is, just in case I approve of X. Moreover, according to simple subjectivists X is good *because* it is approved of by the speaker. Hence SS must be read from right to left: the right-hand side explains why the left-hand side obtains.

A potential problem for simple subjectivism is best put aside early on. This is the worry that it generates contradictions. Suppose I approve of X and you do not. I say, 'X is good' and my judgement is correct. You say, 'X is not good' and your judgement is also correct. So it looks like X is both good and not good, which is a contradiction. This objection disappears, however, if we take simple subjectivism to be a version of relativism, in the sense explained in Section 2.3. It is a mistake, the simple subjectivist will say, to think that there is a single frame of reference by which we can assess the judgement that X is good. X is good relative to me but not good relative to you – either because the words 'X is good' express different claims in our mouths or because they express the same claim which must be assessed from different points of view (mine and yours).[24]

Relativism aside, simple subjectivism is simple in at least three ways. First, it says that the psychological states that matter for ethics are the states of a *single individual*. Second, that the psychological states that matter are *actual* rather than hypothetical. Third, it does not employ *normative* language on the right-hand side of its biconditional. In Section 4 I consider versions of subjectivism that are not simple in each of these ways. For now, I focus on the simple view.

3.2 Variations

This subsection is a digression. In it, I consider some variations on simple subjectivism. Each of these variations is simple in the sense just defined, yet distinct from SS. After introducing them, I will not assess them, since I think each succumbs to one or other of the objections to simple subjectivism given

---

[22] Chapter 15.

[23] In what follows I typically leave the 'morally' implicit, but it is important to note that SS is not intended as an account of what is, say, aesthetically, prudentially, or instrumentally good.

[24] An early discussion of the relativism in subjectivism is Moore (1912: ch. III).

below. The process of applying those objections to these variations I leave as an exercise for the reader.

We can generate variations on simple subjectivism by fiddling around with the right-hand side of SS. There are three possible choice-points, each marked with a set of braces here:

SS*. X is good iff {X} {is approved of by} {the speaker}.[25]

Consider first possible substitutions for {X}. It seems inevitable that the right-hand side of SS* must involve X in some sense, otherwise the goodness in question would not be X's goodness; but it is not necessary that it include X *just by itself*. For example, suppose what one approved of was not X but *loving X*. This suggests:

SS$_{love}$. X is good iff loving X is approved of by the speaker.

Other possible substitutions for {X} include desiring X, admiring X, commending X, praising X, cherishing X, valuing X, and so on.

There are a similar range of possible substitutions for the second set of braces in SS*, including ... is desired by ..., ... is loved by ..., ... is admired by ..., ... is cherished by ..., ... is valued by ..., and so on. One mustn't be confused by the fact that this list is similar to the list of possible substitutions for the first set of braces. For although the lists are similar, the substitution-points are distinct. This can be seen by the fact that a similar item can be substituted at both points. Suppose, for example, we begin with SS* and substitute {desiring X} for {X} and {is desired by} for {is approved by}. Then we get:

SS$_{desire.}$ X is good iff desiring X is desired by the speaker.

In other words, X is good just in case the speaker desires to desire X. Desiring to desire may seem like a technical notion, but it should be psychologically familiar. I wish I desired to save the planet, or work for world peace, but, unfortunately, I fail to be gripped by such complex issues. That is to say that I desire to desire to save the planet, but I do not actually desire to save the planet (I disappoint myself). Even more familiar are cases where we have desires that we do not want to have – a desire to smoke, for instance, or to watch gruesome videos. In both cases we have desires *concerning* other desires – what philosophers call 'second-order' desires. SS$_{desire}$ says that what is good depends on our second-order desires.[26] This is in fact much more plausible than the first-order view that says what is good depends on what we desire. On the first-order view smoking would be (morally) good for those who desire it, but on

---

[25] Henceforth I abbreviate 'if and only if' as 'iff'.   [26] For discussion see Moore (1903: §13)

the second-order view it would not (assuming that smokers do not desire to desire to smoke).

The third place for possible variations concerns the third set of braces in SS*. According to simple subjectivism the individual whose psychology determines the moral facts is the speaker (hence it is sometimes called 'speaker' subjectivism, for example in van Roojen 2015: 99–101). Yet a possible variant holds that the person whose psychology matters is a person who is *involved* in some way with X. Since there are many ways in which a person can be *involved* with X, there are many possible variations at this point. For example, suppose X is an object or quality that a person can *possess* (such as a vase or knowledge). Then one might hold:

> SS$_{possessor}$. X is good iff X is approved of by the person who possesses it.

Alternatively, suppose that X is an action that a person can perform (such as helping other people or dancing). Then one might hold:

> SS$_{agent}$. X is good iff X is intrinsically approved of by the person who performs it.

On this view helping a neighbour across the street will be good only if the person helping intrinsically approves of doing so. It will not be good, for example, if they are only helping because they are wanting to be seen to help.

One final variation on simple subjectivism is worth noting. Suppose one holds – as seems plausible – that different people approve of different things and for different reasons. To simplify, suppose that Bob approves of actions X, Y, and Z, because they produce pleasure, whereas Greta approves of actions A, B, and C, because they produce equality (of resource). One might then hold that, whenever someone calls something good, what they are saying is not that they approve of it but that it *has the feature in virtue of which they approve of things*. So when Bob calls something good he is saying that it produces pleasure and when Greta calls something good she is saying that it produces equality. This view is sometimes called indexical relativism, and it can be summarised as:

> IR. X is good iff X is F (where F is the property in virtue of which the speaker approves of things).[27]

Strictly speaking, IR is not a version of subjectivism, since it does not hold that moral judgements are made true by psychology. Rather it holds that the moral judgements ascribe non-moral properties, but precisely which property any particular judgement ascribes is determined by the speaker's attitudes. IR

---

[27] For discussion see Dreier (1990, 2009).

does, however, have a somewhat similar profile to subjectivism, in terms of the senses of 'subjective' set out in Section 2.2. IR is also relativist in the first way distinguished in Section 2.3: as with the judgement that 'I am male', the claim made by the judgement varies according to who is speaking.

3.3 The Status of SS

Let's return to simple subjectivism:

SS. X is good iff X is approved of by the speaker.

What is the *status* of this biconditional? *Why* is it true that X is good just in case it is approved of by the speaker? There are at least two answers to this question, which generate two distinct versions of simple subjectivism. Roughly, according to the first answer, SS is true because the right-hand side is an *analysis of the judgement* made on the left-hand side. This generates *analytic* simple subjectivism – a claim about the meaning of moral judgements. According to the second answer SS is true because the right-hand side *identifies the property* ascribed by the left-hand side. This generates *empirical* simple subjectivism – a claim about the identity of moral properties.[28] In the next two subsections, I say a little about each of these views.

3.3.1 Analytic Simple Subjectivism

A judgement (such as 'X is good') deploys certain concepts (such as 'good'). An analysis of a judgement is an analysis of the concepts it deploys. An analysis of a concept is an account of the connections between that concept and others in our overall scheme of thought. A classic example of judgement-analysis would be the analysis of 'X is a bachelor' as 'X is an unmarried man'. This connects the concept of *bachelor* to that of *unmarried* and *man*. Such analyses are generally considered *a priori* – we discern them not by empirical investigation but by considering the role these judgements play in our scheme of thought (roles that may not be obvious or transparent).

If we take SS as an analysis of the judgement that X is good, it is an account of the *meaning* of 'X is good' and therefore a first-order semantic theory (see Section 1.4.1). On this view SS is an attempt to understand or elucidate moral judgements and their content, an 'account of what moral thought and talk is really about' (Milo 1995: 204), namely speaker psychology.

---

[28] Theories of this type are also sometimes called 'metaphysical' or 'synthetic'. For discussion see Blackburn (1993a).

3.3.2 Empirical Simple Subjectivism

According to empirical simple subjectivism, by contrast, SS provides an account of the *property* ascribed by the judgement X is good. (In Section 2.2 I called this 'property analysis' but this is potentially misleading, so I shall drop the term 'analysis' here and speak instead of property identity.) On this view the property of *goodness* is identical with the property of *being approved of by the speaker*, and hence the judgement that X is good will be correct just in case X is approved of by the speaker. Yet the word 'good' doesn't mean the same as 'approved of by the speaker'. Rather the word 'good' refers to a property, and that property, as it turns out, happens to be the property of being approved of by the speaker. A classic analogy for this type of theory would be the claim that 'water' refers to the property of *being H_2O*, even though 'water' does not mean the same as 'H_2O'. Rather these are two distinct ways of referring to what turns out to be the same property. Such accounts are generally considered *a posteriori*. For example, we discover that water is H_2O through empirical investigation rather than reflecting on the concept of water. Empirical simple subjectivism makes a similar claim: we discover, empirically, that the property of goodness is identical with the property of being approved of by the speaker.

If we take SS to be a claim about the identity of the moral property of goodness, it remains just that, and not a claim that gives the *meaning* of any judgements that ascribe that property. Thus, unlike its analytic counterpart, empirical simple subjectivism is not a first-order semantic theory. Rather it is an account of the correctness conditions of moral judgements, of what sort of facts make moral judgements correct.

3.4 Final Characterisation of Subjectivism

The distinction between analytic and empirical versions applies to more than just simple subjectivism. Most generally analytic versions of subjectivism hold that moral *concepts* can be analysed in terms of concepts of psychological attitudes ('attitudinal concepts'), whereas empirical versions hold that moral *properties* are identical with psychological, attitudinal, properties. The difference is that moral concepts are elements of thought, whereas moral properties are elements of facts. Note that, on both views, what makes moral judgements correct is facts about attitudes. So both analytic and empirical versions of subjectivism accept that the correctness conditions of moral judgements are attitudinal, but they have different views as to *why* this is so. For analytic subjectivists it is because moral judgements *mean the same as* attitudinal judgements. For empirical subjectivists it is because moral judgements ascribe moral properties, and these properties are identical with attitudinal properties. A definition of subjectivism that encompasses both views is:

> S**. The semantic function of moral judgements is to express beliefs whose correctness conditions are attitudinal. Hence moral commitments are beliefs with attitudinal correctness conditions.

Assuming that judgements inherit the correctness conditions from the beliefs they express, S** entails that moral judgements have attitudinal correctness conditions, that is, whether or not they are correct necessarily depends on the attitudes of some (actual or possible) people.

S** is my preferred general characterisation of subjectivism.[29] Any more particular version will say something about the particular attitudinal correctness conditions of moral judgements. So, for example, a subjectivist might claim that the correctness condition for the judgement that X is good is that the speaker approves of it – this is simple subjectivism, captured by the familiar:

> SS. X is good iff X is approved of by the speaker.

Analytic and empirical subjectivism then have different stories to tell about why the judgement on the left-hand side has the correctness conditions specified by the right-hand side. According to analytic simple subjectivists this will be because the judgement on the right-hand side *has the same meaning as* the judgement on the left-hand side, that is, they will accept:

> AS. 'X is good' *means* 'X is approved of by the speaker'.

According to empirical subjectivism the judgement on the left-hand side of SS has the correctness conditions specified by the right-hand side because the former judgement ascribes the property of goodness to X, and that property turns out to be the property of being approved of by the speaker. Thus empirical simple subjectivists accept:

> ES. The property of goodness *is identical with* the property of being approved of by the speaker.

To summarise: most generally, subjectivists in ethics accept S**. Particular versions of subjectivism will also accept biconditionals such as SS and supplement them with claims of the form AS (if they are analytic subjectivists) or ES (if they are empirical subjectivists).

---

[29] The difference between S* and S** is that the former refers to the contents of beliefs (what they are about), whereas the latter refers to their correctness conditions. These can come apart, as in the case of the belief that this stuff is water (which is correct iff this stuff is H_2O but whose content does not involve H_2O). S* – my initial characterisation of subjectivism – captures only analytic versions.

3.5 Can Simple Subjectivism Accommodate the Features of Moral Practice?

Let's consider each feature (from Section 1.4.2) in turn.

3.5.1 Practicality

Moral judgements are practical in at least two respects: they provide answers to practical questions and they are necessarily (if defeasibly) connected to appropriate motivation.

3.5.1.1 Motivational Internalism

Take this second aspect first – the thesis of 'motivational internalism'. According to analytic simple subjectivism when I judge that 'X is good' I am judging that I approve of X. Approval is a type of motivation. Therefore, according to this view, there is a necessary connection between judging that something is good and *making a judgement about* motivation. However, making a judgement about motivation, even one's own motivation, does not entail actually having that motivation (even ruling out abnormal circumstances such as psychopathy, jadedness, or general tiredness). So what we *do not* have here is a necessary connection between moral judgement and *actual* motivation. Hence analytic simple subjectivism does not accommodate motivational internalism.

To make this vivid, consider the case where I *think* that I approve of giving money to charity but in fact I do not (I have deceived myself into thinking I am a nice guy). Suppose I judge 'I approve of giving money to charity'. According to analytic simple subjectivism I have judged that giving money to charity is good, but I do not have the appropriate motivation to give money to charity, because I am deceived about my own approvals. It follows that, unless supplemented, simple subjectivism does not generate a necessary connection between moral judgements and appropriate motivation. It generates only a connection between *true* moral judgements and appropriate motivation, whereas motivational internalism applies to both true *and false* moral judgements.

Analytic simple subjectivists might reply that people are never wrong about their own approvals – these matters are 'transparent'. Supposing that judgements of goodness are judgements about our own approvals, and that we are never deceived about our own approvals, it follows that, whenever I judge that something is good, I will actually approve of it, and hence be appropriately motivated. The required connection between moral judgement and motivation is restored.[30]

---

[30] See van Roojen (2015: §6.1.3) and Dreier (1990: 16–17).

This reply has three serious drawbacks, however. First, the assumption of transparency is implausible – just ask any good therapist. Second, even if we grant transparency, it is at best an empirical hypothesis, so the connection between moral judgements and motivation it generates is partly empirical and not necessary. Finally, a serious drawback of granting transparency is that together with analytic simple subjectivism it entails that our judgements of goodness are infallible. If judgements of goodness are judgements about our own approvals, and if we are never incorrect about our own approvals, then our judgements of goodness are never incorrect; but this is surely too strong: we are sometimes wrong about what is good. Hence it seems that, in both its bare and supplemented form, analytic simple subjectivism cannot accommodate motivational internalism.

3.5.1.2 Normative Meaning

Consider the second aspect of the practicality of moral judgements. Such judgements are practical insofar as they answer practical questions, questions about what to do and feel. According to analytic simple subjectivism moral judgements are a type of psychological judgement, more particularly they are judgements about one's own attitudes. The question, therefore, is whether judgements about one's own attitudes answer practical questions, and it appears that they do not. Because being told, or agreeing, that one approves of a certain thing does not help answer the question of whether *to* approve of it.

A general version of this point is sometimes called the 'autonomy of the normative' or 'So what?' argument.[31] The thought is that mere descriptions of the world cannot determine answers to practical questions. Whenever we are told that the world *is* a certain way, it always makes sense to ask the question 'So what?' More precisely, we can ask: 'So what if the world is that way? How does that determine what *to do* about it?' According to analytic simple subjectivism moral judgements are descriptions of the way the world is. They are descriptions of the way the world is *with respect to our own psychology*, but these are descriptions, nonetheless. So the general point about the autonomy of the normative applies: 'So what if my psychology is a certain way? What does that matter to the question of what to do about it?' This suggests that moral judgements, construed as a species of psychological judgements, do not have the right type of normative meaning to answer practical questions.

---

[31] Classic statements can be found in Johnston (1989: §IV) and Blackburn (1998: 70, 90–1). A more recent version is in FitzPatrick (2019). There are also complex connections between this point, Hume's dictum about the impermissibility of deriving an 'ought' from an 'is', and Moore's charge of naturalistic fallacy. See Sinclair (2019).

The analytic simple subjectivist might reply: when you judge that something is good, you're judging that you approve of it; and in most (though not all) cases when you judge that you approve of something, you actually approve of it. Hence, in most cases, when you judge that something is good, you will approve of it; and approving of something is surely relevant to the practical question of what to do about it. Hence analytic simple subjectivism makes moral judgements relevant to practical questions after all.

Yet this reply doesn't capture the fullest sense in which moral judgements answer practical questions. In Section 1.4.2.1 I drew a distinction between judgements that *foreclose* practical questions and judgements that *answer* them. If I am an irredeemably compulsive gambler, my judgement that a venue has slot machines forecloses the question of whether to go, but it does not answer it. Now, even granting a strong connection between judging that one approves of something and actually approving of it, to judge that one approves of something will at best *foreclose* the question of what to do about that thing. In other words, if judging that one approves of something reliably suggests that one does approve of it, then the judgement that one approves will make the question of whether to approve somewhat moot. It will not answer that question, however, since whether to approve is not determined by whether one actually approves. Thus, like my judgements about slot machines, judgements about my own approvals at best foreclose practical questions rather than answer them. Hence analytic simple subjectivism cannot accommodate the normative meaning of moral judgements.

3.5.1.3 Empirical Simple Subjectivism and Practicality

Things are not looking good for simple subjectivism. Perhaps they will go better if we switch from analytic to *empirical* simple subjectivism. This makes a claim not about the meaning of moral judgements but about the nature of the properties ascribed by such judgements. It says that the property of goodness just is the property of being approved of by the person making the judgement, but the judgement does not mean the same as a judgement describing that approval.

Consider whether this view accommodates motivational internalism. According to empirical simple subjectivism when an agent judges that X is good, and when their judgement is correct, they will approve of X. Thus there is a connection between *correct* judgements of good and appropriate motivation. However, this is not the connection that motivational internalism demands, which is a connection between *all* judgements of good and appropriate motivation, whether those judgements are correct or not (even a neo-Nazi is, unfortunately, normally motivated in accordance with their moral judgements).

Moreover, it is difficult to see how empirical simple subjectivism *could* secure such a connection. This is because, according to this view, moral judgements express beliefs (about attitudes), and beliefs seem to be disconnected from motivation in the way set out in Section 1.3 – beliefs by themselves do not provide any motive to action.

This last argument is not conclusive (though it is part of a venerable tradition against subjectivism and other 'cognitivist' theories; see, for example, Snare 1975 and Smith 1994). It is open to the subjectivist to modify their view to the claim that moral judgements express beliefs about moral properties, *as well as* correlated motivating attitudes. So, for example, one might claim that the judgement that X is good *both* expresses a belief that is correct just in case the speaker approves of X *and* expresses that approval. The former would make this a version of subjectivism, the latter secure the necessary tie between moral judgements and appropriate motivation. This would be to accept a type of *hybrid* theory that claims that moral judgements express both beliefs (with attitudinal correctness conditions) and attitudes.[32] However, despite appearances, such hybrid theories still fail to accommodate motivational internalism. For, according to such views, it is logically possible to express a belief about moral properties without expressing the correlated attitude (though it may not be possible to do this using our current moral terms). Such expression would seemingly count as a moral judgement, since it is a judgement expressing a belief about moral properties; but, as a singular belief, it would not be necessarily connected to motivation in the way motivational internalism demands.

Let's return to empirical simple subjectivism. I have argued that it cannot accommodate motivational internalism, but what about normative meaning? The trouble here is that empirical simple subjectivism doesn't tell us *anything* that elucidates or gives the meaning of moral judgements – it only tells us that moral judgements express beliefs with attitudinal correctness conditions. Insofar as the phenomenon of normative meaning just is a phenomenon concerning *meaning*, empirical versions of subjectivism do nothing to accommodate it. Moreover all other types of judgements that express beliefs seem to have precisely the wrong type of meaning to answer practical questions (this is just the point about the autonomy of the normative again). Thus empirical simple subjectivism also fails to accommodate either aspect of the practicality of moral judgements.

3.5.1.4 Some Caveats

In the interests of balance, it is important to note that many of the arguments just given could be questioned at crucial points. For example, one might question the

---

[32] See Dreier (1990), Sinclair (2007), and Tresan (2006).

idea that the connection between moral judgement and motivation is necessary, as opposed to common (Section 3.5.1.1). Perhaps the 'So what?' argument begs the question against subjectivism by assuming a notion of normative meaning that it has no right to assume (Section 3.5.1.2); and perhaps the hybrid subjectivist can defend their theory by pointing out that the strict separation between beliefs and attitudes rests on an ungrounded 'Humean' theory of motivation (Section 3.5.1.3). Unfortunately, there is not space to pursue all of these replies here, so I leave that exercise to the reader.[33]

A further strategy in defence of simple subjectivism would be to turn revisionary (see Section 1.4.4). At various points in this discussion, I have suggested that simple subjectivism can secure *a* connection between moral judgements and motivation, just not quite the connection we were seeking. It is therefore open for the simple subjectivist to claim that, although there are *some* senses of practicality that their theory cannot accommodate, there are other senses that it can, and these accommodations are enough to provide a plausible reconstruction of moral judgement. To assess this move, we need to consider the following questions: How important to the overall practice of morality are the senses of practicality that simple subjectivism accommodates? How important are the senses that it *cannot* accommodate? In particular are the senses of practicality that simple subjectivism *cannot* accommodate *essential* to moral practice? If they are, then simple subjectivism must be condemned as changing our moral practice beyond reasonable recognition. If they are not, then simple subjectivism can survive as a tolerably revisionary account of moral judgements. These are difficult issues that I cannot settle here, but I hope to have given the reader enough material to begin that assessment for themselves.

3.6 Disagreement

Let's turn now to the second feature of moral practice in need of accommodation. Moral disagreement is disagreement that is genuine, moral, and *sui generis* (Section 1.4.2.2). Can simple subjectivism accommodate it?

Seemingly not. In fact not only does simple subjectivism fail to accommodate moral disagreement, it renders such disagreement impossible. This is a bad result for a theory hoping to map the contours of actual moral practice.

To see why, begin with analytic simple subjectivism. Suppose Alice approves of X and judges 'X is good'. Bob does not approve of X and judges 'X is not

---

[33] For an argument against the necessary connection suggested by motivational internalism see Brink (1989: ch. 3). For the suggestion that the 'So what?' argument begs the question, see Section 4.2.2.3. For scepticism about the Humean theory see McDowell (1978) and Dancy (1993).

good'. This looks like a genuine moral disagreement, focused on the issue of X's goodness, but there is no moral disagreement here, if analytic simple subjectivism is true. For, according to that theory, when Alice judges that X is good, she means that she – Alice – approves of X; and, when Bob judges that X is not good, he means that he – Bob – does not approve of X. Both these things are true (moreover both Alice and Bob could recognise that both are true). So Alice's judgement is true, as is Bob's; but then these judgements cannot disagree with each other, *a fortiori* they cannot constitute a case of moral disagreement.

This shows that analytic simple subjectivism cannot accommodate cases like Alice and Bob as cases of moral disagreement, but I also just claimed that analytic simple subjectivism renders moral disagreement *impossible*. Diagnosing *why* the example of Alice and Bob is not a case of moral disagreement will help support this stronger claim.

Alice and Bob are not disagreeing with each other. Why? Because in making their moral judgements, they are talking about different things. Alice is talking about her attitudes and Bob is talking about his. Generalising, according to analytic simple subjectivism, whenever *anyone* makes *any* moral judgement, they are talking about their *own* attitudes. Moreover, no one can use moral judgements to talk about anything else, since moral judgements just are a way of talking about *one's own* attitudes (just like I cannot use the word 'I' to talk about you). So there is no single subject matter that different people making moral judgements could thereby be talking about and disagreeing over. Moral judgements are inherently introspective and personal, and as such cannot reach out to a shared topic over which people might disagree. This is why moral disagreement is impossible, according to analytic simple subjectivism.

Is there any way that the analytic simple subjectivist might reply? Here is one possibility. They might say:

> OK, look, I agree that Alice and Bob are not disagreeing over any matter of fact. In making moral judgements both express beliefs that are true. So there is no disagreement in judgement or belief between them. However, there remains a *different* type of disagreement that *attends* their exchange. In particular there is disagreement *in attitude*. Roughly, disagreement in belief occurs when two or more people have beliefs such that the truth of one rules out the truth of the other. Disagreement in attitude occurs when two or more people have *opposed attitudes* – one approving of an object, for instance, and another disapproving of it. So, although Alice and Bob do not have a disagreement in belief, they still have a disagreement in attitude that *attends* their exchange.

Call this the attendant attitudinal disagreement manoeuvre, or AADM.[34]

AADM is neat but ultimately does not help the subjectivist accommodate moral disagreement. There are at least two reasons why. First, some cases of apparent moral disagreement will not, according to subjectivism, involve any attendant attitudinal disagreement. In fact the case of Alice and Bob is like this. Alice approves of X and Bob does not. This is not an attitudinal disagreement, since Alice and Bob do not have opposed attitudes – rather Alice has an attitude that Bob lacks. Second, AADM doesn't capture the full force of moral disagreement. As I argued in Section 1.4.2.2, moral disagreement is disagreement that not merely attends moral judgements but *focuses* on them. AADM denies this. It accepts that moral disagreement is not focused on moral judgements (both Alice's and Bob's moral judgement are true, according to AADM, and both Bob and Alice can recognise this) but is, instead, enshrined in the attitudinal disagreement that sometimes attends these judgements. This is to accommodate disagreement in a sideshow tent, not the big top.

Does empirical simple subjectivism fare any better here? Seemingly not. According to empirical simple subjectivism both Alice and Bob have made moral judgements that are true, since whether or not their judgements are true depends on their own attitudes. Given this, it is hard to see how Alice and Bob can disagree, insofar as disagreement seems to require that at least one of their judgements is false. Neither will AADM help, since again this will at best capture an attendant disagreement, not one focused on the moral judgements themselves. Neither version of simple subjectivism, therefore, can accommodate genuine moral disagreement.

3.7 Mind-Independence

According to the claim of mind-independence elucidated in Section 1.4.2.3, the moral facts about a thing do not, in general, depend on our thoughts about, or attitudes towards, that thing. Murder is wrong, to be sure, but it is not wrong because I (or you, or anyone) disapprove of it. At any rate this seems to be a common assumption of moral practice in need of accommodation. Can simple subjectivism accommodate it?

Seemingly not. In fact simple subjectivism seems committed to four implausible claims concerning the mind-*dependence* of moral facts. To bring out these claims, it is easier to switch to the simple subjectivist account of 'bad', which is:

---

[34] The classic statement of the disagreement problem is Moore (1912: chs III–IV). A good discussion of AADM is Köhler (2012), and the first problem for it mentioned in this subsection comes from Schroeder (2008: 17). A related manoeuvre is to claim that Alice and Bob's disagreement is meta-linguistic, that is, it concerns whether to use the term 'good' in a way that ties its meaning to Alice's attitudes or that ties its meaning to Bob's attitudes (see Plunkett and Sundell 2013). It is an interesting question whether this meta-linguistic manoeuvre suffers the same fate as AADM.

SS$_{bad}$. X is bad iff X is disapproved of by the speaker.

Suppose I disapprove of torture and say, 'Torture is bad'. According to SS$_{bad}$ my judgement is correct, but bad things follow from this.

3.7.1 The Euthyphro Contrast

At *Euthyphro* 10a, Socrates asks:

> Is the holy holy because the gods love it? Or do the gods love it because it is holy?

Similarly we may ask:

> Is the bad bad because we disapprove of it? Or do we disapprove of it because it is bad?

Simple subjectivism seems committed to the first clause. As noted in Section 3.1, simple subjectivism intends its biconditionals be read right to left: it is *because* the psychological conditions mentioned on the right-hand side obtain that the moral facts mentioned on the left-hand side obtain. Thus, if simple subjectivism is true, I must accept:

> (1) Torture is bad *because* I disapprove of it.

Yet this claim is manifestly implausible. It also seems to contradict the thought that if something is bad it is bad because of its own features, not our reactions to it. For example, torture is bad in part because of the pain and emotional scars it causes its victims.

To this last point the subjectivist might reply: 'We disapprove of torture because of these features. So torture is bad because we disapprove, but we disapprove because of the emotional scars. By the transitivity of explanation, torture is bad because of these scars.' But even if this reply is successful, it doesn't address the previous point that simple subjectivism commits us to claims like (1).

3.7.2 The Modal Problem

If torture is bad because I disapprove of it, then it seems to follow that, if I did not disapprove of it, it would not be bad (see Schroeder 2008: 16–17). Thus simple subjectivism also commits me to:

> (2) If I did not disapprove of torture, it would not be bad.

Similarly, I must accept that, if I approved of torture, it would be good. Yet these are also implausible claims – I cannot make torture good by changing my mind.

3.7.3 Contingency

Our approvals and disapprovals are contingent. I like the Packers and dislike the Patriots, but things could have been otherwise. This is also true for my disapproval of torture. Although this is a deeply engrained attitude, it is possible that I do not have it – one can imagine a suitably sketchy upbringing that leads to me approving of torture. Yet, if the moral facts depend on our (dis)approvals and if these are contingent, it follows that the moral facts are contingent too. Hence simple subjectivism commits me to:

> (3) Torture is not necessarily bad.

What goes for the moral status of torture goes for all other moral facts as well – all moral truths are only ever contingent. Again, this is implausible. (Note that the implausibility need not rest on the particular example of torture. Any moral system that holds at least one moral truth to be necessary will be in tension with the claim that all such truths are contingent.)

3.7.4 Epistemology

Necessary truths require a necessary epistemology. It is because philosophers deal with necessary truths that they get away with investigating from their armchairs. It is in fact quite mysterious how we come to know necessary truths, but it is commonly assumed that, whatever that method is, it typically does not involve empirical investigations such as those carried out by psychologists. If, however, as simple subjectivism holds, moral truths are contingent truths about the psychology of speakers, it seems to follow that we should investigate them by investigating our own psychological states. More particularly:

> (4) To investigate whether torture is bad, we should investigate our own psychological states.

This is also implausible. We do not investigate moral matters by introspection. We come to our moral judgements by investigating and reflecting on the features of the things being judged. Simple subjectivism therefore generates the wrong 'moral gaze' (see Blackburn 1993a: §5). It directs our attention inwards towards our own mental states rather than outwards towards the features of the objects we are evaluating.

3.7.5 Replies

It seems that simple subjectivism commits us to implausible claims about the way moral facts depend on, and change with, our psychology. How might the simple subjectivist reply? As in Section 3.5.1.4, revisionism is one possible strategy.[35] The simple subjectivist could accept that their theory commits us to claims like (1)–(4) and that these claims are not how we generally think of moral truths; but they could argue there is minimal mutilation done to moral practice if we simply revise how we generally think of moral truths and come to see them as subjectivism suggests – contingent and dependent on psychology. As in the previous case, to assess this strategy we would need to consider the centrality of the revised elements to moral practice as a whole.

An alternative strategy is to revise not our moral practice but our subjectivism. That is, we could move away from simple subjectivism towards more complex versions. This is the strategy explored in Section 4.

4 Complex Subjectivism

Simple subjectivism is simple in three ways: it focuses on *individual* psychology, *actual* psychology, and psychology *not* specified in *normative* terms. We can generate complex versions by revising each of these features. We can 'go communal' and suggest that what matters for ethics is not the psychology of individuals but the psychology of groups. We can 'go ideal' and suggest that what matters for ethics are not actual mental states but the mental states people *would have* in some hypothetical conditions. Or we can 'go normative' and suggest that what matters are the mental states that would be *appropriate* or *virtuous*. In this section I assess each of these views.

4.1 Communal Subjectivism

Morality is other people's business, something that people do to each other. If I disapprove of your loud parties, ask you to stop them, organise a neighbourhood petition, and seek a court injunction against you, then I manifest a moral stance. Morality is thus communal, part of the mechanisms by which we regulate behaviour within societies. Taking this aspect to heart may suggest that moral judgements are made true not by facts of individual psychology but by facts of *group* psychology. This is communal subjectivism.

It will be useful to focus on one particular version, namely:

CS. X is good iff X is generally approved of by people in the speaker's group.

Here the speaker's group might be her fellow citizens, those who share her upbringing, those who feel the same way as her, or those who are party to the

---

[35] A different response to some of these problems is to 'rigidify' one's subjectivism, so that what matters for ethics are not attitudes per se but actual attitudes. For both the move and a reply see Lewis (1989: 132–3).

same agreements and conventions as her. Gilbert Harman accepts a view of this kind for some moral judgements. He holds that

> morality arises when a group of people reach an implicit agreement or come to a tacit understanding about their relations with one another.

And

> moral judgments . . . make sense only in relation to and with reference to one or another such agreement or understanding.[36]

Very roughly, Harman's view is that X is good just in case the speaker and those in her group have generally agreed to promote it. Since whether or not such an agreement is in place is a matter of group psychology, this is a version of communal subjectivism.

Although communal subjectivism departs from simple subjectivism by being focused on groups rather than individuals, it is relativist in the same way (hence why some, such as Harman, call it 'moral relativism'). According to communal subjectivism, whether a moral judgement is correct depends on the frame of reference in play: the judgement that torture is bad may be correct relative to one group but incorrect relative to another. Like its simple counterpart, communal subjectivism also comes in analytic and empirical versions (see Section 3.3). According to the former, the version of communal subjectivism captured by CS is a claim about the meaning of judgements of good; according to the latter it is a claim about the identity of the property of goodness.

4.1.1 Assessing Communal Subjectivism

In this Element we are assessing metaethical theories by asking whether they accommodate the three features of moral practice outlined in Section 1.4.2. Does communal subjectivism fare any better than simple subjectivism on these scores?

4.1.1.1 Practicality

Let's consider practicality first. Again this has two dimensions: motivational internalism and normative meaning. When it comes to the former, communal subjectivism appears no better off than simple subjectivism. In its analytic form communal subjectivism says that, when I judge that X is good, I am judging that X is generally approved of by my group; but judging that X is generally approved of by my group does not entail that I approve of X (even putting aside abnormal circumstances), both because my judgement might be incorrect and because I may be an atypical member of my group. As before, *if* it were the case that no

---

[36] Harman 1975: 3.

one was ever mistaken about their group's approvals, then it would follow that (unless one was atypical), whenever one judged that X is good, one approved of X. Yet this communal transparency assumption is even less plausible than its individual counterpart and has exactly the same drawbacks (see Section 3.5.1.1).

Familiar problems also infect communal subjectivism when it comes to normative meaning. Descriptions of communal attitudes seem to be the wrong type of things to answer practical questions. Faced with a description of the attitudes of the local populace, one can always retort: 'So what? Why should their attitudes be relevant to what I do? I've always been a rebel, after all.' Descriptions of group attitudes may serve to *foreclose* practical questions (peer pressure can be a powerful motivator), but this is distinct from *answering* such questions. Social psychology seems to have the wrong kind of content to answer practical questions.

Finally, empirical versions of communal subjectivism seem to face difficulties similar to those faced by empirical versions of simple subjectivism. Motivational internalism is hard to accommodate because communal subjectivism still takes moral judgements to express beliefs, which are motivationally disengaged; and normative meaning is hard to accommodate because the empirical subjectivist says very little about the meaning of moral judgements, other than that they ascribe moral properties.

4.1.1.2 Disagreement

Communal subjectivism has a much better time accommodating moral disagreement, and its improvement over simple subjectivism in this regard has been one of its main attractions. Simple subjectivism suffered here because, on its view, moral judgements can only be used to speak about the speaker's own mental states, so cannot establish a shared subject matter to disagree about. Communal subjectivism breaks this bind, because it holds that moral judgements are used to speak about the attitudes of the *group*. As long as two speakers are members of the same group, they can disagree about those attitudes. This is what moral disagreement amounts to according to communal subjectivism.

Although this is certainly an improvement on simple subjectivism, there are limitations. For still, on this view, where two or more speakers are from *different* groups, there can be no moral disagreement between them. Suppose Alfonso and Betty belong to different societies and meet on an international cruise. People in Alfonso's society approve of X, and people in Betty's society do not. Alfonso judges that 'X is good', and Betty counters 'X is not good' (conversation on cruise ships is often more interesting than this, but only marginally). Again there seems to be moral disagreement here, but according to communal subjectivism both judgements are correct, since both successfully describe the attitudes of the judge's society. So communal subjectivism cannot accommodate this disagreement. (Side quest for the reader: might AADM, from Section 3.6, help?)

The communal subjectivist might reply: 'Look, I admit that my theory cannot accommodate the thought that members of different groups can morally disagree. This is a revisionary cost. But still, my theory *can* accommodate a great deal of moral disagreement, insofar as it is disagreement within groups.'

The core of this reply is surely correct: in accommodating *some* moral disagreement, communal subjectivism is less revisionary than simple subjectivism, which accommodates none; but it also highlights a further question: how much of the important moral disagreement we see is disagreement *within groups*, and how much of it is disagreement *between* groups? Alfonso and Betty's seems to be a disagreement between groups, so cannot be accommodated by communal subjectivism. Yet we can also imagine cases where members of the same group disagree over which set of collective attitudes *should* be adopted, not just over what those attitudes currently are. Such disagreements would seem to be moral disagreements but cannot be if communal subjectivism is correct. The remaining issue, then, is whether the types of moral disagreement that communal subjectivism secures are the types necessary for a tolerably revisionary account of moral practice.

4.1.1.3 Mind-Independence

When it comes to accommodating mind-independence, communal subjectivism seems to suffer similar defects to simple subjectivism. Suppose, as seems plausible, that torture is generally disapproved of in our society. Then, communal subjectivism commits us to:

> (1*) Torture is bad *because* it is generally disapproved of in our society.

Again, however, this seems implausible: the badness of torture does not depend on a popular vote.

By making moral facts depend on the actual approvals and disapprovals of those in our society, communal subjectivism also seems to force us to accept:

> (2*) If torture were not generally disapproved of in our society, it would not be bad.

Since general disapproval of torture is itself a contingent state of affairs, we can again infer:

> (3) Torture is not necessarily bad.

Again these claims are implausible. We could not, for example, make the world a better place just by brainwashing everyone so that they no longer disapproved of torture. Nor is it easy to conceive of a situation where torture as we currently understand it exists but is not bad. In these respects communal subjectivism seems just as problematic as simple subjectivism.

Turn finally to epistemology. How, according to communal subjectivism, are we supposed to discern moral facts? Since they are facts of communal psychology, we discern them in the way we discern communal psychology, by investigating the psychological states of our group. Thus communal subjectivism seems to entail:

> (4*) To investigate whether torture is bad, we should investigate the psychological states of our group.

Again, however, this seems to mistake the proper direction of the moral gaze. We seek increased moral understanding not by examining ourselves but by examining the objects of our moral judgements. Communal subjectivism seems to reduce moral investigation to the situation of a nervous board member, who has no idea of the correct answer to the current crisis but anxiously looks to the people either side of him so that he can quickly agree with whatever they say.

To summarise, when it comes to accommodating our three features of moral practice, communal subjectivism is in one way slightly preferable to simple subjectivism (disagreement) and in two ways just as bad (practicality and mind-independence). This is progress but of a minimal kind. Perhaps the problems, then, arise from the elements shared between simple and communal subjectivism. Both theories hold that what matters for ethics are *actual* psychological states, of individuals or groups. Yet perhaps this is a mistake, and we would do better to pursue a version of subjectivism that grounds ethical truths on *hypothetical* mental states. This is the approach taken by idealising subjectivism.

4.2 Idealising Subjectivism

A joke can be outrageous, even if it not presently causing any outrage. Metaphysics can be tiresome, even if not currently sending anyone to sleep. In both cases, the property depends not on our actual responses but on the responses we *would* have, or are *disposed* to have, in certain conditions. Perhaps moral properties are like this. Perhaps goodness, for example, depends not on actual approval but on the ways we are disposed to approve, or would approve, in certain conditions. On this view something can be good even if no one presently approves of it, so long as the disposition is there. Such a view is more plausible than simple and communal subjectivism insofar as both of those other views entail that, were no one to approve of anything, nothing would be good. (On those views the property of goodness is like the property of *being harmless* possessed by the Weeping Angels in TV's *Doctor Who* – it's only there so long as you are looking at it.) By contrast the view we are now considering allows that things can be good even if no one is currently approving of them, so long as people are *disposed* to approve of them in certain conditions. This theory captures the thought that morality is made for us – insofar as it suits responses we are capable of – but not made immediately *by* us.

4.2.1 Varieties

One version of idealising subjectivism is:

> IS$_w$. X is good iff {X would be approved of} by {the speaker} when {confronted with or thinking about X}.

Something like this view was defended by Edward Westermarck, who wrote:

> the moral concepts intrinsically express a tendency to feel a moral emotion of either approval or disapproval ... [hence] a judgment which contains such a concept may be said to be true if the person who pronounces it actually has the tendency to feel the emotion in question with reference to the subject of the judgment.[37]

Like all versions of subjectivism discussed so far, this is a version of relativism. According to it, judgements of goodness are only ever correct relative to the context of who is making them.

We can move towards non-relative versions by abstracting from Westermarck. The right-hand side of IS$_w$ involves three variables, each highlighted by a pair of braces: an attitudinal response directed at X (call it R), an individual who possess that attitude (call them P), and a circumstance in which that attitude arises (call it C). Thus a more general schema for idealising subjectivism is:

> IS. X is good iff {P} would have {R} in {C}.

Equivalently, we could say that X is good iff {P} is disposed to have {R} in {C}. One might worry that the term 'X' does not appear on the right-hand side of these biconditionals, but in fact it is there, just buried within the attitude R, which is *directed at* X.[38]

---

[37] Westermarck 1932: 141–2.

[38] In this section I talk of 'dispositions' and responses we 'would have'. For problems translating this into conditionals see Blackburn (1993a: §2). I also deliberately do not express IS as:

IS*. X is good iff X is disposed to elicit {R} from {P} in {C}.

IS* suggests that goodness depends on how people react to *samples* of X, as opposed to depending on which X-directed attitudes people have in conditions that need not involve samples of X. For this point, and the way in which it marks a decisive break between this treatment of moral properties and popular 'response-dependent' treatments of 'secondary' qualities, see

Variations of idealising subjectivism (sometimes also called 'dispositional theories of value') can be generated by different substitutions for {P}, {R}, and {C}. For example, {P} could be: the speaker, the speaker's group, Donald Trump, most of us, everyone, all possible beings of a certain kind, the experts, the ideal observers, etc. {R} could be: approval of X, desire for X, desire to desire X, love of X, admiration of X, etc. And finally {C} could be: when confronted with X, thinking about X, fully imagining X, in full knowledge of the facts (about X), when thinking dispassionately, impartially and consistently (about X), ideal conditions (for X), etc.

Westermarck's version of idealising subjectivism is relative because the right-hand side of the biconditional contains a relative phrase, namely 'the speaker', which refers to different people in different contexts. To construct an absolute version we simply need to replace such phrases. For example:

IS_T. X is good iff Donald Trump would approve of X when imagining it.

On this view goodness is not relative, because whether or not something is good depends on just one possible frame of reference, namely Donald Trump. IS_T is ridiculous, of course, and only a supreme narcissist would believe it, but it is helpful to illustrate the possibility of non-relative versions of subjectivism. Here is a more plausible version:

IS_F. X is good iff any ideal observer would approve of X when in full knowledge of all the non-moral facts and when thinking impartially, dispassionately, and consistently.

An ideal observer is someone who has full knowledge of the non-moral facts and who thinks impartially, dispassionately, and consistently. (This illustrates how the line between what goes into {P} and what goes into {C} is somewhat arbitrary). IS_F is absolutist because according to it whether or not X is good depends on one frame of reference, namely the ideal observer. IS_F is close to the 'ethical absolutism' defended by Roderick Firth (1952) and has several similarities to the account of rightness defended by Peter Railton (1986).

Another variety of idealising subjectivism is defended by David Lewis (1989):

IS_L. X is good iff we would desire to desire X in conditions of full imaginative acquaintance with X.

Being fully imaginatively acquainted with X is imagining vividly and thoroughly what it would be like if X were realised. It is different from, and less onerous than, having full knowledge of X. Having full knowledge of pleasure,

---

Lewis (1989: 123–4). For more on moral properties and the analogy with secondary qualities see Johnston (1989) and Wright (1988).

for instance, would require detailed scientific knowledge of its physiological bases, whereas being imaginatively acquainted with it would not. Lewis argues that imaginative acquaintance is a better standard than full knowledge, since full knowledge of anything (or indeed, everything) may extinguish all positive attitudes, which by IS_F would entail that nothing is ever good.

A further interesting feature of Lewis's idealising subjectivism is its conditional relativism. The 'we' in IS_L could refer to just me and you, to me and those in my street, me and those in our town, or city, or society, or even me and all possible human beings. As the scope of the 'we' expands, so does the strength of the claim being made: it is much stronger to claim that everyone in our society would desire to desire X than just to claim that me and you would. So when I say that X is good, which 'we' am I referring to? Lewis's view is that there is often no answer to this question. As he explains:

> How much am I claiming? – as much as I can get away with. If my stronger claims were proven false ... I still mean to stand by the weaker ones. So long as I'm not challenged, there's no need to back down in advance; and there's no need to decide how far I'd back down if pressed. What I commit myself to is *conditionally relative*: relative if need be, but absolute otherwise.[39]

In other words, moral judgements are always made relative to the context of some group or other, but precisely which group need not be obvious when we are making those judgements. Our judgements test the waters, so to speak, to see how many of our fellows are fellow-feelers.

One final source of variation among idealising subjectivists concerns the familiar question of the *status* of their biconditionals. According to Firth, for example, idealising subjectivism is an *analysis* of moral judgements. Lewis and Railton offer *partial* analyses of our moral concepts but accept these may not capture all of the elements we normally take to be involved – their views are therefore partly revisionary. Brower (1993), by contrast, offers idealising subjectivism as an empirical identification of moral properties.

4.2.2 Assessing Idealising Subjectivism

Is any version of idealising subjectivism plausible?[40] I have already noted one advantage, but how does it fare when it comes to accommodating the features of practicality, disagreement, and mind-independence (Section 1.4.2)?

---

[39] Lewis 1989: 129.

[40] One objection to idealising subjectivism that I do not discuss is given in Enoch (2005). Enoch argues that idealising subjectivism can give no good reason to privilege hypothetical over actual attitudes.

I will break with my previous habit and take these features in reverse order, starting with mind-independence.

4.2.2.1 Mind-Independence

Like all versions of subjectivism, idealising subjectivism intends its biconditionals be read right to left. On Firth's view, for example, X is good *because* any ideal observer would approve of it in conditions of full information and when thinking impartially, dispassionately, and consistently. If we switch the example to the badness of torture, Firth's view would seem to be committed to:

> (1**) Torture is bad *because* any ideal observer would disapprove of it in ideal conditions.

How implausible is this? It is certainly a distinct type of claim to the ones entailed by simple and communal subjectivism – that is, (1) and (1*). According to those claims, the badness of torture depends on our *actual* attitudes, but (1**) does not say that: it says that this badness depends on the attitudes ideal observers *would* have in ideal conditions. The idealising subjectivist might well argue that, although claims like (1) and (1*) are in tension with common-sense assumptions about moral facts, claims like (1**) are not – rather common sense simply takes no stand on the issue of the dependence of moral facts on *idealised* responses (see Brower 1993: 242–4). The idealising subjectivist can, in addition, point out that (1**) is *consistent* with the thought that torture is bad in part because of the pain and emotional scars it leaves – since we can suppose that ideal observers would disapprove of torture for precisely these reasons. There is even an argument to be made that (1**) is supported by common-sense assumptions, such as the thoughts that morality is made for us and that moral truths are always within reach (if not of everyday folk, then at least of some accessible idealisation of them).

Idealising subjectivism also seems to fare better when it comes to the modal problem. Idealising subjectivism denies that moral properties depend on our actual responses. It therefore denies that, were our *actual* attitudes to change, the moral facts would change. What it does entail, though, is claims like the following:

> (2**) If the ideal observers in ideal conditions did not disapprove of torture, then torture would not be bad.

This claim is less implausible than the parallel claims (2) and (2*), made by simple and communal subjectivism. According to those claims, if the actual responses of the speaker or her group were to change, the moral facts would change; and part of the problem was that the actual responses of speakers and their groups might be extremely fickle – they could change even if little else did.

Consider, by contrast, what the world would have to be like in order for *ideal observers* not to disapprove of torture. The ideal observers are not fickle: their attitudes are formed after careful consideration of the nature of the objects they are evaluating. Therefore, in order for ideal observers *not* to disapprove of torture, it seems that torture itself would have to be very different from how we currently understand it to be. Yet if torture were very different from how it now is, it is not obviously clear that it *would* be bad. (Imagine torture that causes no pain.)[41] In other words, claim (2**) may actually be rather plausible. Once one understands what would have to be the case in order for the antecedent to hold, it is quite plausible that in those circumstances the consequent would hold as well.

It seems, then, that idealising subjectivism is more plausible than other versions of subjectivism when it comes to the Euthyphro contrast and the modal problem. What about contingency? Simple and communal subjectivism seemed to entail that it is at best a *contingent* truth that torture is bad. Does idealising subjectivism have the same consequence? For Firth's version of idealising subjectivism, at least, that would depend on whether it is *necessary* that ideal observers would disapprove of torture. There is certainly nothing logically necessary about this. Further, what the ideal observers would disapprove of seems to be a matter of psychological fact, and psychology is contingent. Lewis (1989: 132–7) explicitly bites this bullet, admitting that such contingency is inevitable. It therefore seems as if idealising subjectivism, like its simple and communal subjectivism, commits us to:

> (3) Torture is not necessarily bad.

However, perhaps the idealising subjectivist can make this bitten bullet somewhat palatable. For they can argue that, although torture is not necessarily bad, it could not easily *not* be bad. For in order for torture not to be bad it would have to change from how we currently understand it to be – change enough so that the ideal observers no longer disapprove of it. This requires much more radical change to the effects of torture than is required just for *actual* people no longer to disapprove of it (since actual people can be fickle).

Consider the final issue included under the heading of mind-independence: the correct direction of the moral gaze. In normal circumstances, we investigate moral matters by looking outwards into the world, and the nature of things being evaluated, rather than looking sideways at the attitudes of our group or inwards

---

[41] Perhaps this stretches the bounds of sense. If so, one could swap 'torture' for 'hitting people on the head with hammers'. If ideal observers did not disapprove of *that*, perhaps that would be because it no longer hurt.

to our own psychology. Simple and communal subjectivism failed to accommodate this phenomenology. Can idealising subjectivism do better?

Seemingly, yes. Consider first how one might go about finding out whether, in ideal conditions, ideal observers would approve of X. The most obvious strategy would be to turn oneself into an ideal observer, place oneself in ideal conditions, and only then look inwards to see what one approves of (see Lewis 1989: 116). This is a kind of 'Try it, you might like it' approach, and following Lewis I call it the 'canonical method'. Now suppose that the ideal conditions involve knowledge of, or imaginative acquaintance with, X. Then getting oneself into those conditions will require investigating the nature of X or imagining what X would be like were it realised. These are outward-facing investigations – concerned with the nature of X – but they are relevant for discovering ethical truth, according to idealising subjectivism, because we need to complete them to get ourselves into the ideal conditions, and thence see what our reactions in such conditions would be. Thus idealising subjectivism is perfectly compatible with claims like:

(4**) To investigate whether torture is bad, we should investigate the nature and consequences of torture.

This account of moral epistemology brings a further advantage to idealising subjectivism, namely its ability to explain ethicists' otherwise puzzling reliance on thought experiments. Any student of ethics will be familiar with such experiments (concerning violinists, fat men on bridges, people stuck in mineshafts, and so on) which are designed to generate an intuitive moral verdict that can be used to support or undermine an ethical theory. Yet how does imagining hypothetical cases manage to tell us anything about ethical truth? Further, does the method of thought experiment provide *a priori*, or *a posteriori*, knowledge of such truths? Idealising subjectivism provides simple answers here. Imagining hypothetical cases tells us about ethical truth because ethical truth is determined by the reactions of ideal observers, and in imagining those cases we are trying to approximate the position of ideal observers. Thought experiments therefore provide a type of *a posteriori* knowledge – knowledge of what ideal observers would approve of in ideal conditions; and this is ethical knowledge because ethical truths just are truths about what ideal observers would approve of in ideal conditions. This account of moral epistemology can in fact be turned into a positive argument for idealising subjectivism, since more than any other theory (especially those that appeal to 'rational intuition' and the like) it seems able to explain why the methods we ordinarily deploy in ethics are *good* methods for ascertaining moral facts.

4.2.2.2 Disagreement

Things are looking up for idealising subjectivism, but can it accommodate moral disagreement?

Absolutist versions have the upper hand here. On these views moral disagreement is disagreement concerning the dispositions of ideal agents. These dispositions provide a common subject matter regarding which all those making moral judgements can be in dispute. Relativist versions of idealising subjectivism, on the other hand, face exactly the same problem that troubled communal subjectivism: where moral judgements are relativised to groups, people from distinct groups cannot morally disagree. Whether this approach is tolerably, or unbearably, revisionary of the actual moral disagreements we see is an exercise I leave to the reader.

Lewis's conditional relativism might also help here. According to Lewis, moral judgements are always made relative to groups, but it can be indeterminate, and certainly not settled at the time the judgement is made, which is the relevant group. Lewis (1989: 128) suggests that there might be good pragmatic reasons to assume that the people one is apparently disagreeing with are making judgements relativised to the same context, even if, ultimately, they are not. For example, if you and I are disagreeing about the badness of torture, it may suit both of us to suppose that our judgements are relativised to the same group, since without that assumption there would be no point in either of us engaging with the other; and it may matter to both of us what the other thinks about the morality of torture (insofar as it might affect which politicians get elected, for example, or what goes on in the neighbourhood basements). In this way idealising subjectivism can claim both that much moral disagreement is genuine and that we can understand why sometimes we assume there to be genuine moral disagreement, when in fact there is not.

4.2.2.3 Practicality

Consider finally what idealising subjectivists might say about the practicality of moral judgements. Can they first accommodate motivational internalism? Analytic versions will claim that moral judgements are judgements *about* the motivational (attitudinal) dispositions of ideal agents; and empirical versions will say that moral judgements are made true by facts about the motivational dispositions of ideal agents. Yet in neither case will there be a necessary connection between someone making a moral judgement and their being appropriately motivated. The problem for idealising subjectivism here is exactly the same as the problem for communal and simple subjectivism. Note that the term 'ideal' can be somewhat misleading in this context. As Michael Smith (1994) has argued, it is certainly more rational to have the motivations that you think a *better* version of yourself would have or endorse, so if moral judgements are about the motivations or endorsements of *better* versions of oneself, a type of motivational internalism can be retained. However, as discussed here, idealising subjectivism makes no such claim – it claims only that moral judgements have correctness conditions specified in terms of certain types of agent, for example ones who are fully imaginatively acquainted with the object of evaluation. (Smith's view is best considered a version of normative subjectivism, which I discuss in Section 4.3.)

There is, however, one way in which idealising subjectivism might improve on these other versions. As we saw, idealising subjectivists tend to claim that there is a *canonical method* that we are advised to follow when forming moral judgements; and it seems that there is a necessary connection of sorts between forming judgements *via this canonical method* and being appropriately motivated. This is a weaker connection than that required by motivational internalism (which is a connection between *all* moral judgements and appropriate motivation) but it may be close enough to make the resulting theory tolerably revisionary.

To explain this weaker connection, return to the canonical method which Lewis describes thus:

> to find out whether something is disposed to give response R under conditions C, you can put it in C and find out whether you get R.[42]

In the case of moral judgements R is an attitude of approval (or disapproval) and C are ideal conditions. So suppose you use this method to determine whether X is good. You put yourself in ideal conditions and you come to approve of X. Suppose that, after stepping out of the ideal conditions, you retain that approval and come to judge that X is good. It follows that, if you have formed your judgement that X is good in this way, you will approve of X, that is, be appropriately motivated towards it. Generalising, idealising subjectivism seems to secure the following necessary connection between moral judgement and appropriate motivation:

> Iffy. Necessarily, if an agent judges that X is good, and if she has formed that judgement via the canonical method, and if she has retained her attitudes from the ideal conditions, then (in normal circumstances) she will approve of X.[43]

For comparison the relevant version of motivational internalism is:

> MI. Necessarily, if an agent judges that X is good, then (in normal circumstances) she will approve of X.

---

[42] Lewis 1989: 116.   [43] See Lewis 1989: 116.

As its name suggests, Iffy provides a weaker connection between moral judgement and motivation than MI; but the idealising subjectivist can argue that, when it comes to the assumptions of practicality embedded in ordinary moral practice, there is little to choose between them. If that is right, then idealising subjectivism promises to accommodate the only connection between moral judgements and motivation that needs accommodating.

Let's turn finally to the issue of normative meaning. Can idealising subjectivism accommodate this? Unfortunately, it seems not. For just like simple and communal subjectivism, idealising subjectivism faces the 'So what?' argument. According to idealising subjectivism, moral judgements are either judgements concerning or judgements made true by the attitudinal dispositions of certain people in certain circumstances. However, for any such description it seems open for a deliberating agent to say: 'So what if such-and-such people in so-and-so circumstances would have this-and-that attitude? How does that determine how to respond to X, in the here and now?' Content concerning hypothetical psychology, just like content concerning actual psychology, seems to be the wrong sort to answer practical questions.

At this late juncture I want to note one possible reply that the subjectivist – any subjectivist – might make to the charge that their theory cannot accommodate normative meaning (see Railton 1986: §5). Normative meaning is meaning that answers practical questions. There are ways and ways of answering practical questions, however. Suppose I am considering whether to leave the party and you tell me that my bus will leave soon. Not wanting the long walk home, I pack up and go. Your judgement seems, in some sense, to have answered my practical question, but does that mean that your judgement has normative meaning? That would seem to be an overreaction – it is a simple description of fact, after all, and only seems to have practical relevance insofar as it engages with some of my contingent concerns (e.g. to avoid a long walk). Now perhaps, the subjectivist might argue, moral judgements are practical in just this way: they engage with existing concerns. Perhaps, furthermore, this is *all there is* to normative meaning, and there is no further sense in which a judgement, any judgement, can answer practical questions. (Pure normative meaning is an illusion, one might say.) On this approach moral judgements possess the only type of normative meaning worth seeking – the type that engages with existing concerns.

This is a potentially powerful reply that I do not have space to explore here, but again the way to assess it should be clear: we would need to consider whether the sense of normative meaning this reply captures is a tolerable, or intolerable, revision of the sense assumed by our actual moral practice. (For example, are there cases where moral judgements have normative meaning whose force cannot be tied to existing concerns?)

4.3 Normative Subjectivism

It's time to consider one final type of subjectivism. The best way to approach it is to consider how it differs from idealising subjectivism.

Idealising subjectivists endorse some instance of the following:

> IS. X is good iff {P} would have {R} in {C}.

Note that there are several ways in which this could be problematically circular (see Blackburn 1993a: §4). Suppose first that we substitute for {R} the judgement that X is good. Then we get:

> IS_1. X is good iff {P} would judge that X is good in {C}.

Taken as an *analysis* of the judgement that X is good this is circular, because the very judgement we were trying to analyse appears on the right-hand side. Taken as an empirical account of the property of goodness it faces the problem that it is hard to specify {P} and {C} in non-moral terms. For example, one plausible suggestion would be:

> IS_2. X is good iff impartial judges would judge X to be good once they have grasped all the correct moral principles.

Yet then we have only identified goodness by employing explicitly moral notions ('the correct moral principles'), which is circular.[44]

There are other potential circularities lurking within IS. Suppose we agree that the relevant attitude is approval of X and that the relevant substitutions for {P} and {C} are ideal observers and ideal conditions. Then we get:

> IS_1. X is good iff ideal observers would approve of X in ideal conditions.

Now theories that fit this pattern are unproblematic insofar as the 'ideal observers' and 'ideal conditions' can be specified independently of the concept of 'good'. For Firth, for example, ideal observers in ideal conditions have full knowledge of all the non-moral facts and think impartially, dispassionately, and consistently. For Lewis, ideal observers have full imaginative acquaintance with X. In both cases we can know what the ideal observers and ideal conditions look like, without thinking in terms of 'good'. Contrast the following view, which specifies the 'ideal' observers and conditions in terms of good itself:

---

[44] For this objection see Wright (1988), discussed in Miller (2003: ch. 7).

IS$_C$. X is good iff people who are infallible detectors of goodness would approve of X in perfect conditions for detecting goodness.

Both as an analysis of the judgement, and an identification of the property, this is circular, because the term or property we were hoping to analyse – 'good' or goodness – is used or referred to on the right-hand side.

Suppose, however, that we identify the conditions relevant to goodness not in terms of goodness itself but in terms of *another moral property*. One common thought, for example, is that virtuous people are those that love good things. Twisting this around, we might think that the good things are those that are loved – or at least approved of – by the virtuous people. This would generate something like:

> V. X is good iff virtuous people would approve of X in morally ideal conditions.

Here 'good' does not appear on the right-hand side, so circularity is avoided, but other moral terms do, namely 'virtuous' and 'morally ideal'.

Other versions subjectivism that fit this pattern are:

> M. X is good iff X *merits* approval.
> A. X is good iff approval of X would be *appropriate.*
> F. X is good iff approval of X would be *fitting.*

Whether or not approval is *merited, appropriate,* or *fitting* is not a matter of how things are (or at least not a matter of how things are in the sense that my being over six-foot tall is a matter of how things are). Rather it is a matter of how things *should* be, how they would *ideally* be, or how they *ought* to be. Philosophers sometimes use the phrase 'normative' to refer to judgements and facts that are 'fraught with ought' in this way. Hence versions of subjectivism that employ normative terms on the right-hand side are versions of *normative* subjectivism.[45]

Normative subjectivism has some advantages over other subjectivisms. It accommodates the practicality of moral judgements insofar as it takes moral judgements to be a species of normative judgement and it is plausible to think that normative judgements are both necessarily connected to appropriate motivation and apt to answer practical questions ('Why should I write a thank-you card?'; 'Because it would be fitting'). It accommodates moral disagreement insofar as it takes it to be disagreement concerning what is appropriate or fitting;

---

[45] These are sometimes also called 'non-reductive' versions of subjectivism. Seminal versions are McDowell (1985) and Wiggins (1987).

and it accommodates mind-independence insofar as it claims that moral facts such as X's goodness depend not on our actual attitudes, nor on the attitudes we would have in some hypothetical situation, but only on the attitudes we would have in some *normatively ideal* situation. This is just to claim that some moral facts depend on other normative facts, which is quite unobjectionable. (It is quite common to hold, for example, that wrongness depends on badness, or what we ought to do depends on whether the consequences of our actions are good.)

There are, however, some problems. First, normative subjectivism is unhelpful if our task is to understand not just a particular type of moral judgement – such as judgements of good – but all moral or normative judgements. This is because normative subjectivism gives an account of some moral judgements (such as judgements of good) in terms of other normative judgements (such as judgements of appropriateness, or fittingness, which may in turn be analysed in terms of *reasons* or some other normative notion). Normative subjectivism will therefore be unhelpful for someone hoping to understand the practice of normative judgement in general, even if it is helpful for someone hoping to understand what type of normative judgement moral judgements are. The theory is like a theory of the colour orange that explains it as an amalgam of two other colours (red and yellow): useful if you understand what those other colours are, but useless if you do not understand colours at all.

Second, normative subjectivism seems to undermine one of the key motivations for subjectivism, namely naturalism (Section 1.2). One aspect of naturalism is the thought that all the properties that exist are natural, that is, specifiable in terms amenable to the natural sciences, or some future improvement thereof. Normative subjectivism, however, claims that moral judgements express beliefs about the *appropriateness* or *fittingness* of attitudes and thus ascribe such properties. Therefore, this view seems committed to holding that there are fundamentally normative properties such as *appropriateness* and *fittingness*. This seems unfriendly to naturalism, insofar as neither current science nor any expected improvement of it seems to countenance such properties.

Third and finally, normative subjectivism may invite an unwelcome relativism, insofar as whether or not approval (or disapproval) is 'fitting' cannot be referred to an objective standard (see Milo 1995: 183). Defenders of normative subjectivism tend to argue that there are standards of appropriateness and fittingness for attitudes but that they are only discernible from within a particular framework of attitudes and feelings, and there is no 'Archimedean point' that justifies the adoption of one framework over another. This leaves the account open to the possibility of debased or abhorrent attitudinal frameworks, from the perspective of which it really is appropriate to approve of torture (say) or disapprove of helping people. Whether or not torture was bad would then be relative to whichever attitudinal framework one was judging from.

4.4 Conclusion

No version of subjectivism is completely unobjectionable. The first three versions we considered – simple, communal, and idealising – all come close to securing motivational internalism but none get all the way. Simple versions render moral disagreement impossible. Communal and idealised versions fail to accommodate disagreement in all cases. Simple subjectivism also seems to entail implausible claims about the dependence and variability of moral facts and shares with communal subjectivism a worryingly self-centred moral epistemology. Idealising subjectivism does better here insofar as it can explain why we often look outwards towards objects, rather than inwards at ourselves, when searching for moral truths. Normative subjectivism has its own distinct problems.

One common response to the objections raised was to turn revisionary. This is to accept that subjectivism is incompatible with a certain feature of moral practice but to suggest that moral practice can proceed equally effectively without that feature. Yet this revisionary approach has drawbacks of its own. First, once the subjectivist is willing to revise certain features of moral practice, it is hard for them to argue against other views based on *their* supposed inability to accommodate such features. For example, it will be hard for a revisionary subjectivist to argue that *expressivism* is implausible because *it* is revisionary. Second, any revisionary metaethical theory gives a substantial hostage to fortune. For if a non-revisionary theory of moral practice should be developed, the revisionary theory will be at an automatic disadvantage. For these reasons subjectivists are well-advised not to play the revisionism card too early.

5 Expressivism

In Section 1.4.1 I defined expressivism as:

> E*. The semantic function of moral judgements is to express attitudes. Hence moral commitments are attitudes.

On this view when you say 'Murder is wrong' you express disapproval of murder, and this explains why 'Murder is wrong' means what it does. Further, when you think or accept that murder is wrong, what is going on in your head is that you disapprove of murder. This is sometimes called the 'Boo! Hooray!' theory – since such disapproval might just as well be expressed by shouting 'Down with murder! Boo!'

The aims of this section are threefold. First, to introduce some real expressivists. Second, to refine the definition of expressivism. Third, to consider whether expressivists can accommodate the three features of moral practice outlined in Section 1.4.2.

5.1 Expressivists

Expressivism has rarely enjoyed the status of orthodoxy. Most people who write about it are critics. Many feel it was decisively refuted in the early 1960s by the so-called Frege–Geach problem. (This is the problem of explaining, in expressivist-friendly terms, how sentences such as 'Murder is wrong' can have the same meaning even when they do not express disapproval, for example when we say 'If murder is wrong then attempted murder is wrong' or ask 'Is it really the case that murder is wrong?') Yet since the turn of the twenty-first century interest in expressivism has increased. Whether this is down to some fundamental insight, or the failure of alternatives, is a matter I leave to historians.[46]

No doubt, though, expressivism's longevity is partly down to the few brave souls who have defended it in print. An early example, from 1923, is Ogden and Richards:

> This peculiar ethical use of 'good' is, we suggest, a purely emotive use. When so used the word stands for nothing whatever, and has no symbolic function. Thus, when we so use it in the sentence, 'This is good,' we merely refer to this, and the addition of 'is good' makes no difference whatever to our reference ... [I]t serves only as an emotive sign expressing our attitude to this, and perhaps evoking similar attitudes in other persons, or inciting them to actions of one kind or another.[47]

Note already two features of expressivism or 'emotivism' that supplement E*. First, a claim about the *practical purpose* of expressing attitudes. Speakers express attitudes to *evoke* attitudes and actions in others. Second, a claim about what moral words *do not* do: they do not add to our reference or denote properties. These negative aspects of expressivism came to the fore in the next generation of expressivists, such as A.J. Ayer, who wrote in 1936:

> [I]f I say to someone, 'You acted wrongly in stealing that money,' I am not stating anything more than if I had simply said, 'You stole that money.' In adding that this action is wrong I am not making any further statement about it. I am simply evincing my moral disapproval of it. It is as if I had said, 'You

---

[46] Every serious student of expressivism should study the Frege–Geach problem. I put it aside here partly because it receives excellent discussion elsewhere (e.g. Schroeder 2010) and partly to provide contrast with those discussions in a way that illuminates the wider project of expressivism. For my own attempt at a solution see Sinclair (2011).

[47] Ogden and Richards 1923: 125.

stole that money,' in a peculiar tone of horror, or written it with the addition of some special exclamation marks. The tone, or the exclamation marks, adds nothing to the literal meaning of the sentence. It merely serves to show that the expression of it is attended by certain feelings of the speaker.[48]

On Ayer's view moral judgements merely express attitudes; they do not *state* or *assert* anything. They also have 'no literal significance', 'no objective validity', and cannot be true or false. Moral concepts are not even real concepts, according to Ayer, but 'pseudo-concepts'. It follows that there is no such thing as moral disagreement, since in moral confrontations neither side is 'asserting a genuine proposition' that can be disagreed with.

Ayer was a happy radical, who famously dismissed metaphysics as not just tedious but meaningless. Subsequent expressivists have been less comfortable with Ayer's negativity. Notice that to move from the claim that 'Moral judgements express attitudes' to claims such as 'Moral judgements cannot be true or false' or 'Moral judgements cannot be disagreed with' requires hidden premises about the nature of *truth* and *disagreement*. If we deny those premises, we create space for a position that says that, although the semantic function of moral judgements is to express attitudes, such judgements can still be true and disagreed with. An early proponent of this sophisticated expressivism was Charles Stevenson. Stevenson accepted the core claims of expressivism, according to which:

> although a speaker normally uses "X is yellow" to express his belief about X, he normally uses "X is good" to express something else, namely his approval of X. [The theory] adds that "good," being a term of praise, usually commends X to others and thus tends to evoke their approval as well.[49]

Yet Stevenson also held that these claims are compatible with moral judgements being many of the things that Ayer thought they could not be. For example, he held that moral judgements can be *disagreed with*. According to Stevenson, if Mr. A says 'X is good' and Mr. B says 'X is bad' then they are

> respectively praising and disparaging the same thing ... [T]heir issue [is] a disagreement in attitude – one in which the men initially express opposed attitudes rather than opposed beliefs and thus prepare the way for a discussion in which one of other of their attitudes may come to be altered or redirected.[50]

Stevenson also held that it makes sense for speakers to call moral judgements 'true' since this word merely allows the speaker to reaffirm what has just been said. Thus:

---

[48] Ayer 1936/1990: 110.   [49] Stevenson 1963: 79.   [50] Stevenson 1963: 82.

> When Mr. A says 'Jones ought not to have done it,' and Mr B replies, 'that is true,' ... [Mr. B] too has said, in abbreviated form, the equivalent of 'Jones ought not to have done it.' His 'that is true' permits him as it were to repeat A's remark, thus expressing an attitude ... that is in agreement with A's.[51]

Stevenson was thus an early step on an expressivist path that moves away from the raft of negative claims embraced by Ayer. According to Stevenson moral judgements can be disagreed with and could be true – so long as we understand 'disagreement' and 'truth' in the right kinds of way.

Suppose one takes the possibility of disagreement and aptness for truth as hallmarks of a *realist* practice. (Generically, realism is the view that judgements of a kind express beliefs that represent the world as being a certain way, and that the world often is that way, independent of our thoughts about it, so that such judgements are often true.) Then what Stevenson is doing, in effect, is showing how an expressivist account of moral judgements is compatible with those judgements possessing some of the hallmarks of realism. This makes Stevenson a 'quasi-realist', that is, someone who

> starting from a recognizably anti-realist [e.g. expressivist] position finds himself progressively able to mimic the intellectual practices supposedly definitive of realism.[52]

The 'intellectual practices supposedly definitive of realism' are practices such as moral disagreement and talk of 'true' as applied to moral judgements.

The term 'quasi-realism' was coined by one of the generation of expressivists who came after Stevenson – Simon Blackburn. Blackburn's first contribution was to emphasise the general potential of the quasi-realist programme, namely to enable expressivists to accommodate not merely the features of disagreement and truth but all the features previously thought the exclusive domain of realism (such as talk of moral 'facts', moral 'knowledge', even moral 'descriptions' and 'representations'). The second was to highlight how this quasi-realist man-oeuvre tells us not just about the nature of local practices (e.g. moral practice) but much more generally about the nature of the *features* that such practices sustain. As Blackburn puts it:

> It teaches us a great deal about representation and description to learn that they are so cheap to purchase that even the [expressivist] can have them, along with truth, fact, knowledge, and the rest.[53]

This is one reason why expressivism is one of the more interesting metaethical theories around today. To fully embrace it requires a view not just about moral practice but about the nature of all those notions – such as *truth, fact, knowledge,*

---

[51] Stevenson 1963: 217–18.   [52] Blackburn 1993b: 15.   [53] Blackburn 1993b: 5.

description, and *representation* – that apply to moral and other discursive practices.

Despite these wider ramifications, Blackburn is at heart an expressivist, whose foundational thesis is not appreciably distant from where Ogden and Richards began:

> Expressivism denies that when we assert values, we talk about our own states of mind, in actual or potential circumstances. It says that we *voice* our states of mind, but denies that we thereby describe them . . . When we voice our ethics we have . . . distinct conversational dynamics. People are badgered . . . Emotions are tugged.[54]

For nearly a century, then, the core claims of expressivism have hardly changed. What has changed is our understanding of their explanatory power.[55]

5.2 Refining Expressivism

Expressivism claims that the function of moral judgements is to express attitudes. To further understand this we need to ask: Which attitudes?[56] And how are they 'expressed'? This section addresses these questions.

5.2.1 Moral Attitudes

I have developed a taste for Nutella. I've not always liked it, but just now my clear preference is for Nutella on my morning toast. One might say that I approve of eating Nutella – or at least I approve of *me* eating Nutella, on toast, in the morning. This is an attitude, providing me with a goal and motivation to pursue it, but it is not a *moral* attitude. I do not think that eating Nutella is *morally good*, or that anyone *ought* to eat Nutella. So not all attitudes are moral attitudes.

There appear to be at least four features of moral attitudes that are absent in the case of my nutty preference. First, moral attitudes are partly *other-regarding*. I like Nutella, but this attitude concerns just me and my actions. By contrast, when I think that giving money to charity is good, this applies to not just *my* giving to charity but *your* giving to charity, and *Bob's* giving to charity, and so on. For expressivists, the objects of moral attitudes are *general*.

Second, moral attitudes are *ascended*. I like Nutella but don't care whether *you* like it or not, and I have no view about whether, in general, the liking of

---

[54] Blackburn 1998: 50–1.

[55] Gibbard (1990, 2003) is an expressivist of Blackburn's generation. The next generation includes Barker (2006), Horgan and Timmons (2006), Lenman (2003), and Ridge (2014). For my own attempt at a contribution to the programme, see Sinclair (2021).

[56] Answering this question is sometimes called the 'moral attitude problem'. See, for example, Miller (2003).

Nutella should be encouraged or discouraged. When I think that giving money to charity is good, however, I don't just approve of you and me giving to charity, I approve of you and me *approving* of giving to charity. In other words, my attitude is directed not just at the *action* of giving to charity but at other people's *attitudes towards* that action. Hence moral attitudes are 'ascended': they are directed not merely at actions and objects (the 'first level') but at attitudes towards those actions and objects (the 'ascended level'). Another example: if I think that murder is wrong, I don't just disapprove of murder, I approve of other people *sharing* that attitude and disapprove of those who *do not* share it ('Down with this sort of thing!').

The third difference between moral attitudes and my preference for Nutella is their respective *stability*. Preferences can change, and on a whim. Moral attitudes, by contrast, are typically stable and reflectively endorsed. When I think that giving money to charity is good, typically I endorse this attitude and hold it on the basis of reflection on the nature of its object. Such an attitude will change only if I revise my view about the features of giving money to charity.

This leads to the fourth difference between moral attitudes and basic preferences. When I judge that giving money to charity is good, I strongly imply that I can give a *reason* why it is good; and thinking that giving money to charity is good disposes me to offer such reasons to others, when the issue comes up. Such reasons are the features on the basis of which we approve or disapprove of things. I might say: 'Giving to charity is good, because it saves lives.' Hence moral attitudes are tied to *avowal* in discussion concerning what is good, right, and so on. Yet there is no corresponding aspect of my preference for Nutella. I do not try to impose this on you by offering reasons in its defence. (Thus, as Stevenson emphasised, in comparison with emotions, attitudes are considered, voluntary, and amenable to reason.)

In sum, moral attitudes are distinct from other types of approval and disapproval insofar as they are *general, ascended, stable*, and *tied to avowal*. It is when we start having stable preferences for general patterns of action, preferences that are ascended, and preferences that we attempt to support with reasons, that our attitudes become moral.[57]

The account of moral attitudes just given is a recent innovation that would be alien to expressivists such as Ogden and Richards, and Ayer. Nevertheless it is strongly suggested by claims many expressivists do make about the *practical purpose* of moral judgements. For most expressivists (unlike most critics) are keen to emphasise not only that moral judgements express attitudes but that the

---

[57] The account of moral attitudes outlined here is close to those defended in Björnsson and McPherson (2014), Blackburn (1998: 8–14), Gibbard (1990: 40–54), and Mameli (2013).

purpose or function of that expression is to have an effect on *other people* – to evoke those attitudes in others, spur or deter others from action, and generally to help people *co-ordinate* their reactions. Yet it is only if moral attitudes are directed at other people's attitudes and actions that expressing them will have any hope of altering those reactions. It is only if moral attitudes are stable and reflective that expressing them can hope to lay common ground for stable co-ordination. Further, it is only if moral attitudes are tied to avowal that they can start to influence others through the distinctive mechanisms of moral discussion. Thus the practical purpose of expressing attitudes is an essential part of the expressivist picture insofar as it helps illuminate the nature of moral attitudes.

5.2.2 'Express'

Early expressivists took moral judgements to express attitudes in a similar way to that in which yawning expresses boredom. Yawning *manifests* or *externalises* boredom – it exposes one's inner mental states to others, as is shown by the fact that, on seeing a yawn, one can legitimately *infer* that the person yawning is bored (see Tormey 1971). On this view expression is a relation between a judgement and the mental states possessed by the speaker. For example, in saying 'X is good' Bob expresses *his* moral approval of X.

A little reflection, however, shows that this cannot be the sense of 'express' that expressivism requires. Suppose Greta says 'X is good' *even though she doesn't morally approve of X* – she is being insincere, trying to deceive, or perhaps just confused. Still, her judgement means the same as Bob's; but it cannot mean the same if meaning is explained in terms of mental states expressed (as E* holds), if Greta lacks moral approval (as we are supposing), and if expressing a mental state requires the speaker to possess that state. Hence expressivists must reject this last claim. Greta expresses moral approval of X, even though she does not morally approve of X. Better, therefore, to formulate expressivism as claiming that when someone says 'X is good' they are not expressing *their* moral approval of X but simply expressing moral approval of X. (In the jargon what is expressed is not the speaker's *token* moral approval but the *type:* moral approval.)

This tells us that expression cannot be a relation between the judgements someone makes and their own mental states. So what is it? Mark Schroeder has discussed this issue.[58] According to Schroeder's suggestion, a judgement 'p' expresses a type of mental state M just in case it is part of the assertability conditions of the sentence p that the person who asserts that sentence possesses M. For example, consider my judgement that grass is green. This is a particular

---

[58] See Schroeder (2008: 16–35). Other discussions include Ridge (2014: 109) and Camp (2018).

act of speech that involves uttering the sentence 'Grass is green'. Now this sentence has *assertability conditions*, that is, conditions such that if you do not satisfy them, and assert the sentence, you have misunderstood its meaning. So suppose that I do not believe that grass is green and yet assert 'Grass is green' (and I am not insincere or trying to deceive). It seems that I must have misunderstood what 'Grass is green' means. Hence *believing* that grass is green is part of the assertability conditions for the sentence 'Grass is green'; and that is why my judgement that grass is green expresses the belief that grass is green, according to this account of expression. The moral case proceeds in a similar way. It is part of the assertability conditions of the sentence 'Murder is wrong' that the speaker who asserts it morally disapproves of murder; and this is why this judgement expresses this disapproval.

This account is promising. It allows that speakers can express mental states they do not possess – because, whether or not they possess the state, it remains the case that it is part of the assertability conditions of the sentence used; and this account allows that moral judgements express moral attitudes in just the same way that descriptive judgements (such as the judgement that grass is green) express beliefs. However, there are also problems. First, the notion of 'express' employed by expressivists is supposed to be a notion that *explains* meaning. It better not, therefore, assume an independent notion of meaning; but the current account does just this, since it explains expression in terms of assertability conditions and assertability conditions in terms of meaning. Second, this account seems to suggest that the correctness of moral claims in some way depends on the attitude of speakers. For example, whether it is correct to assert 'Murder is wrong' depends on whether the speaker disapproves of murder – and this seems reminiscent of the objectionable type of mind-dependence that undermined simple subjectivism (Section 3.7). Finally, this account suggests strong and unconventional views about how ordinary descriptive language gets its content. On a standard 'Fregean' account sentences such as 'Grass is green' get their meaning by being associated with *propositions*. On the current account, however, such sentences inherit their meaning from the content of the beliefs they express ('Grass is green' means that grass is green because it expresses a belief with the content: grass is green). As Schroeder emphasises, it seems strange that an account of the expression relation designed to fit the moral context should lead to a radical reappraisal of the meaning of non-moral sentences.[59]

---

[59] Schroeder (2008: 32–5). These objections are not necessarily fatal, and for Schroeder's own further thoughts see Schroeder (2014), but these objections are still, perhaps, sufficiently worrying to motivate interest in the alternative account that follows.

Can the expressivist do better? Here is one suggestion.[60] To express a mental state is to push that state into a public arena of discussion, as a candidate for acceptance or rejection by others. It is to put that type forward as *appropriate* for oneself and others; to advertise a willingness to defend that state for oneself and insist on others sharing it. In expressing a mental state then, one becomes *accountable* for that state, that is, one commits to there being reasons for oneself and one's audience to possess that state, reasons that make that state appropriate. Expressing is presenting-as-appropriate. Thus when a mental state is expressed the issue for discussion is not whether the speaker possesses it but whether *to* adopt that state, and agreement consists in coming to share that state. (Of course whether the speaker possesses the state may be relevant to the issue of whether to adopt it, but the issues are distinct nonetheless.) In the case of beliefs what to believe is a matter of how the world is. In the case of moral attitudes what attitude to adopt is a matter of how to respond to the world. Thus when we express beliefs the topic of discussion is how the world is, and when we express attitudes the topic is how to (collectively) respond to it.

This account raises several questions. First, it appeals to the notion of taking a mental state to be *appropriate* (for oneself and others); but appropriateness might seem a normative notion, undermining any expressivist attempt to explain all normative judgement (recall the problem that affected normative subjectivism in Section 4.3). In response the expressivist can offer an account of what it is to think a mental state appropriate in purely non-normative, dispositional, terms. To think a mental state appropriate is simply to be disposed to defend it in argument, offer considerations in its favour, and to rely on it in deliberation. This leads to a second question: which mental states, and in particular which moral attitudes, are appropriate? For expressivists, to say that a moral attitude is appropriate is to say that the moral judgement that expresses it is correct, so the question of which moral attitudes are appropriate is just the question of which moral judgements are correct, that is, the question of the correctness conditions for moral judgements. This brings us to the issue left over from Section 2.2.

5.2.3 What Are the Correctness Conditions of Moral Judgements?

We already know Ayer's answer to this question: moral judgements do not have correctness conditions at all. We also know the subjectivist's answer: moral judgements have psychological correctness conditions. Yet what makes moral judgements correct according to later versions of expressivism?

---

[60] This account is based on comments by Alston (2000: 51–143), Blackburn (1998: 68–71; 2001: 30), and Barker (2006). See also Sinclair (2021: ch. 3).

First, note that the conditions under which a judgement is correct are distinct from the conditions under which it is *sincere* or unmuddled. If I say 'The Earth is flat' then I am *sincere* only if I believe that the Earth is flat; but my judgement is *correct* only if the Earth really is flat and this is not a matter of what I believe at all. Expressivists will claim that when Bob says 'Murder is wrong' he is sincere only if he morally disapproves of murder. Yet they will also want to insist that whether or not this judgement is correct *does not* depend on whether Bob disapproves of murder but on something else. On what, though?

Here later expressivists make a characteristic move.[61] The question of what makes moral judgements correct is not a question that has a general answer at the level of metaethics. Rather it is a question that must be addressed from within one's particular ethical framework, from within the set of moral attitudes one endorses. So, for example, the question of the conditions under which Bob's judgement that murder is wrong is correct just is the question of the conditions under which murder is wrong; and that is a moral question – a question of which attitudes to adopt and why – not a question of meaning or metaethics. My personal view, like Bob's, is that murder is wrong. Moreover I think that murder is wrong *because* it ends lives – this is the feature in virtue of which I disapprove of murder (and I think you should disapprove of it on this basis too). So, according to me, what makes Bob's judgement correct is that murder ends lives (this is its correctness condition). In saying this I am not making a metaethical claim. I am voicing my moral standard: people ought to take account of the fact that murder ends lives and, on that basis, disapprove of it. So: well done Bob!

Hence I can say that what makes Bob's judgement correct is not any psychological fact about Bob, or about me, and this is true for many moral judgements. In general the correctness conditions of moral judgements are not psychological. In making this general claim, too, I am voicing or summarising my own moral standards; but it is perfectly possible to adopt a set of moral standards according to which moral attitudes are generally appropriate not because of facts about psychology but because of the features of the objects judged. (Indeed this is not only possible but understandable given the practical co-ordinating role of moral judgements – see Sinclair 2008.)

The upshot is this. It is perfectly possible for moral judges of whom expressivism is true to say this: what makes moral judgements correct are features of the objects being judged and not psychological features of the judges. In saying this they are voicing their non-subjectivist moral standards. They are saying, in effect: let's not form our moral attitudes in response to what people think; let's

---
[61] See Blackburn (1984: 217–20; 1998: 68–77, 279–4).

form them on the basis of the features of the things being evaluated! Hence expressivism does not commit moral judges to the view that moral judgements have psychological correctness conditions. In this sense it is not subjectivist.[62]

We can now also address the residual question of whether expressivism is a version of relativism (Section 2.3). I defined relativism as the view that whether a judgement is correct depends on one among a number of possible frames of reference; but, according to me, whether the judgement that murder is wrong is correct depends on one frame of reference, namely the frame that considers the features of murder (such as its tendency to end lives). The same applies for many others of my moral judgements. It is therefore perfectly possible, if expressivism is true, for moral judges to take a non-relativist approach to the correctness conditions of their moral judgements. Thus expressivism doesn't force us to be moral relativists.

I also noted that there are two versions of relativism: one according to which the content of judgements varies with their context of use (the case of 'I am male') and one according to which the correctness of the judgement depends on the context of assessment (the case of 'Bob is moving'). The preceding paragraph suggests that expressivism doesn't commit moral judges to the latter; but the former is also worth considering. According to this relativist view the relevant judgements *make claims about the nature of the world* (e.g. it is a world in which someone is male) but which precise claim is made depends on the speaker's context. Expressivism cannot be a version of this type of relativism, because expressivism denies that moral judgements make claims about the nature of the world. This highlights a further feature of the expressivist account: the denial of possible *analyses* of moral words or concepts. To analyse a word is to express its meaning in simpler, component, parts. According to expressivists, however, moral words play distinctive practical roles in our language and interactions. Hence they cannot be analysed in terms of words that do not play the same type of practical role. Hence expressivists agree with the conclusion of G.E. Moore's famous Open Question Argument, which argues that 'good' cannot be defined. Yet while for Moore this was because 'good' denoted a unique non-natural type of property, for expressivists it is because 'good' plays a unique expressive and practical role.[63]

---

[62] For recent discussions of expressivism potentially collapsing into subjectivism see Schroeder (2014) and Suikkanen (2009).

[63] For connections between expressivism and Moore's Open Question Argument see van Roojen (2019).

5.3 Assessing Expressivism

Can expressivism accommodate the features of moral practice set out in Section 1.4.2? In the next three subsections I suggest it can, to an extent. Afterwards, I consider some objections.

5.3.1 Practicality

The practicality of moral judgements has two aspects. First, moral judgements have normative meaning. Second, moral judgements have a connection to motivation: necessarily, if an agent makes a moral judgement, then, in normal circumstances, she will possess an appropriate motivation. (Where the 'normal circumstances' are just those that exclude cases of psychopathy, jadedness, tiredness, and the like – see Section 1.4.2.1.)

Take this second aspect first. According to expressivism moral judgements express attitudes. To express an attitude is to present it as appropriate for oneself and others. In normal circumstances if one presents an attitude as appropriate for oneself and others, one will possess that attitude; and attitudes are motivations. Hence, if expressivism is true, in normal circumstances, when an agent makes a moral judgement, they will be appropriately motivated. Thus expressivism accommodates motivational internalism.

Let's turn next to the phenomenon of normative meaning. Normative meaning is meaning that answers practical questions; but what does it take for a judgement to answer a practical question? At a minimum, the judgement must be connected to motivation, for it is absurd to think that an agent has answered her practical question of what to do and yet has no motivation to act. Yet this is only a necessary condition, as shown by the example of the gambling addict's judgement that 'The venue has slot machines' (Section 1.4.2.1). A necessary *and* sufficient condition for a judgement to answer a practical question is that the connection to motivation be provided by the meaning of the judgement. The judgement that 'The venue has slot machines' does not provide that sort of connection, because even in the mouth of the addict the meaning of the judgement is explained in terms of the description of the world it offers, a description that in itself entails nothing about motivation. However, moral judgements, construed as expressivists suggest, *do* provide the right sort of connection, because the meaning of a moral judgement is explained in terms of motivating states – moral attitudes. This is not to say that the meaning is explained in terms of those judgements *offering descriptions of motivating states* – that would return us to subjectivism, which, as we saw, has trouble accommodating normative meaning. Rather it is to say that the meaning is explained in terms of motivating states themselves, and their expression. The difference between explaining meaning in terms of *expressing* motivating states and explaining it in terms of *describing* such states is that the latter provides a connection to *possessing* motivation only if the description is accurate, whereas the former provides a connection to possessing motivation in all cases where the judgement is sincere and unmuddled. For expressivists, meaning itself provides a connection to motivation; for subjectivists, meaning provides a connection to a *description of motivation*, and the world must do the rest. Thus expressivism – but not subjectivism – can accommodate normative meaning.[64]

5.3.2 Disagreement

Moral disagreement is disagreement that is genuine, moral, and *sui generis*. The disagreement between Leavers and Remainers (see Section 1.1) is one example. Can expressivism accommodate this?

I have already mentioned Stevenson's approach to disagreement. For Stevenson, moral disagreement is disagreement in attitude, that is, the sort of disagreement which occurs where

> agents have opposed attitudes to the same object – one approving of it, for instance, and another disapproving of it – and when at least one of them has a motive for altering or calling into question the attitude of the other.[65]

According to Stevenson disagreement in attitude is distinct from disagreement in belief and differs from mere differences in taste insofar as it involves interpersonal pressures (the motives for calling others' attitudes into question).

Stevenson's view is attractive. It allows that moral disagreement is genuine insofar as it is disagreement in attitude. Moral disagreement is distinctively moral because moral judgements express attitudes, and moral disagreement is disagreement in just these attitudes (compare Section 3.6). Finally moral disagreement is *sui generis* because disagreements in attitude can outrun agreement in belief. You and I could agree on all of the non-moral features of murder, for instance, and still have differing attitudes towards it.

There are, however, problems with Stevenson's account.[66] First, it implies that there are two fundamental types of disagreement – in belief and in attitude – and fails to explain what unites them under a common kind. Second, it seems to render moral disagreement insufficiently *serious*. According to Stevenson moral disagreement is the same type of disagreement that goes on when

---

[64] For further discussion of expressivism and practicality see Blackburn (1998: 70), Snare (1975), and Sinclair (2007).
[65] Stevenson 1944: 2.   [66] See Ridge (2013).

a couple cannot agree where to eat dinner: they have opposed attitudes and each has a motive to change the other's attitude; but moral disagreement seems much more serious than this.

These problems are not perhaps insurmountable. In response to the first the expressivist can argue that what unifies all disagreements is that they are cases where the relevant mental states cannot collectively fulfil their functions. Two opposed beliefs (e.g. the belief that grass is green and the belief that grass is not green) cannot collectively fulfil their functions, since the function of beliefs is accurate representation, and the world can only be one way (grass is either green or it is not). Likewise, two opposed moral attitudes (e.g. approval and disapproval of murder) cannot collectively fulfil their functions, since the practical function of moral attitudes (and their expression) is to advocate co-ordinated policies of attitude and action, and opposed attitudes advocate incompatible policies. This also provides the material to answer the second problem. The difference in seriousness of moral disputes, compared to disputes about where to eat, is due to the fact that the types of attitudes involved in the former – *moral attitudes* – are psychologically more important, and harder to give up, than preferences about where to eat. So although moral disagreements are 'mere' disagreements in attitude, this is consistent with holding that some attitudes (and the disagreements they engender) are psychologically more important than others.

5.3.3 Mind-Independence

In general the moral facts about a thing do not seem to depend on our thoughts about it. Murder is wrong, but not because we disapprove of it. Rather it is wrong because it ends lives. Can expressivism accommodate these types of mind-independence?

We have already seen how expressivists can make sense of the thought that murder is wrong *because* it ends lives (Section 5.2.3). The key is to understand this thought as an expression of a moral standard, according to which disapproval ought to be formed on the basis of features of actions such as their tendency to end lives. So when I say that murder is wrong because it ends lives, I am highlighting the feature in virtue of which I disapprove of murder, and also the feature in virtue of which I think you should disapprove of murder too.

For similar reasons, it follows that expressivists are *not* committed to claims such as:

(5) If I (or we) did not disapprove of murder, it would not be wrong.

This claim expresses a moral standard according to which we should form our disapproval of murder merely on the basis of disapproving of murder (i.e. on the basis of nothing at all). This is an objectionable moral standard, an objectionable way of forming moral attitudes. Don't form your moral attitudes on a whim (I say), form them on the basis of the actual features of the objects being judged! In rejecting claims such as (5), I express this moral standard.[67]

Similar moves allow expressivists to make sense of the necessity of some moral truths and the proper direction of the moral gaze. According to my moral stance, for instance, murder is wrong because it ends lives; but it is necessary that murder ends lives – murder is just defined as unlawful killing. Therefore murder is necessarily wrong. In making this last claim I am expressing disapproval of murder and pointing out that the feature in virtue of which it is wrong is a necessary feature of it. Finally, if one endorses a set of moral standards according to which moral attitudes are best formed as responses to the actual features of objects (rather than as responses to people's psychology), then it follows that, when deciding which moral attitudes are appropriate, one should examine the features of the objects being judged rather than (say) one's own mental states. The moral gaze is properly directed outwards not inwards (or sideways). Thus expressivism can accommodate moral mind-independence.

5.4 Expressivism and Revisionism

The arguments of the previous two sections are the most controversial in this Element. There are many points at which opponents might object, and readers wishing to pursue those objections should follow the further readings listed in the notes. Yet without getting bogged down in detail, it will be helpful to consider a general objection to such expressivist manoeuvrings, namely that they entail an intolerably revisionist approach (see Section 1.4.4).

The thrust of this objection is as follows.[68] Expressivism can accommodate features such as talk of 'truth' for moral judgements, moral disagreement, and moral mind-independence *only by changing* our common understanding of these features beyond reasonable recognition. So, for example, expressivism accommodates talk of 'true' as applied to moral judgements but only by taking truth to be something other than what it is commonly assumed to be, namely correspondence to the facts. Expressivism accommodates moral disagreement but only by taking it to be a special type of disagreement in attitude, as opposed to the standard understanding of disagreement as disagreement in belief. Finally, expressivism accommodates some of the claims associated with mind-independence but only by reinterpreting them as first-order moral claims about

---

[67] For further criticisms and discussion see Zangwill (1994), Sinclair (2008), and Warenski (2014).
[68] For the objection see Schroeder (2008: ix), Cuneo (2006; 2014: 153–4). For discussion see Sinclair (2012).

the appropriate ways of forming moral attitudes, as opposed to claims about the way moral properties relate to other types of properties. In these and other ways one may feel that expressivism is only accommodating the features of moral practice *when those features are interpreted in a particular (controversial) way.* In other words, expressivists only accommodate cheap simulacra of the features of moral practice, not the real McCoy.

Is this a reasonable objection? That depends, I think, on getting clearer about the precise nature of the features of moral practice. When two speakers have a moral disagreement, for instance, are they assuming that that this disagreement is disagreement in *belief* (as opposed to *attitude*)? Are any moves they make within that disagreement incompatible with interpreting it as a disagreement in attitude? If so, then expressivism seems to be revisionary of these features of our moral practice. If not, however, there is no revision. On this latter alternative expressivism captures all the forms and assumptions surrounding moral disagreement that need capturing. To get clearer about the force of this objection, therefore, requires deeper investigation into the features of moral practice, about which assumptions are made when people make moral judgements, and which assumptions are dispensable to the core activities of that practice.

An opponent of expressivism could also take this objection one step further by arguing as follows. Look (the opponent could say) even putting aside the issue of whether expressivism revises the senses of truth, disagreement, or mind-independence *embedded in our moral practices*, it surely revises the usual way *that philosophers have understood these notions.* So even if expressivism does not revise moral practice, it revises philosophical orthodoxy about the nature of truth, disagreement, and mind-independence; and that is enough to turn us away from expressivism and towards theories that preserve this orthodoxy (such as, perhaps, subjectivism).

There is clearly something in this objection. Orthodox philosophical theories are usually orthodox because they are somewhat successful, so turning to non-orthodox theories risks sacrificing these successes. Sometimes, however, orthodox theories are orthodox for less savoury reasons – for example, because they are the most easily understood or work well in one particular field which has, for contingent reasons, been the focus of philosophical discussion. Given the possibility of such nefarious reasons for orthodox status, we need to be careful about placing the burden of proof too squarely on non-orthodox views. This returns us to the attitude to expressivism evinced by Blackburn: it promises to teach us a lot about the nature of truth, disagreement, mind-independence, and so on. Expressivists will see here a gain in understanding, opponents a threat to well-grounded orthodoxy.

5.5 Conclusion

I have tentatively argued that expressivism can accommodate the features of moral practice mentioned in Section 1.4.2, but note again that there are very many other features of moral practice that I have not discussed. Some of these – in particular, those associated with the Frege–Geach problem – are generally considered to be *very difficult* for expressivists to accommodate. So this section cannot be construed as a complete defence of expressivism; but, as well as giving examples of some expressivist accommodations, it highlights two features of the general programme which the reader may wish to explore further. First, that the expressivist gains when she emphasises the practical, co-ordinating purposes of expressing attitudes (this purpose helped identify the nature of moral attitudes and the seriousness of moral disagreements). Second, that expressivism puts pressure on orthodox notions of truth, disagreement, mind-independence, and so on and thereby forces us to carefully examine the grounds of those orthodoxies. In this sense a radical streak remains at the heart of expressivism.

Glossary

Accommodate. To accommodate a form or assumption is to provide an explanation of why a practice with that form or assumption has arisen and (ideally) to justify that practice carrying on with that form or assumption (Section 1.4.2).

Attitude. A mental state that provides its possessor with a goal and a motivation to pursue that goal (Section 1.3).

Correctness conditions. The conditions under which, necessarily, a judgement is correct (Section 2.2).

Express. To express an attitude or other mental state is to present it as appropriate for oneself and others (Sections 1.3 & 5.2.2).

Expressivism. The view that the semantic function of moral judgements is to express attitudes (Section 1.4.1).

First-order semantic theory. A theory that specifies or gives the meaning of a judgement (Section 1.4.1).

Metaethics. The part of philosophy that addresses general questions about what we are doing when we engage in moral practice (Section 1.2).

Metasemantic theory. A theory that explains the meaning of a judgement (Section 1.4.1).

Moral commitment. The mental state involved in accepting a moral claim, such as the claim that murder is wrong (Section 1.3).

Moral judgement. The particular speech act performed when someone assertorically utters a moral sentence such as 'Murder is wrong' (Section 1.3).

Moral practice. The practice involving the use of moral concepts in thought, language, and interactions with others. It includes making moral judgements, moral deliberation, moral debate, moral argument, and the way these guide our actions (Section 1.4.1).

Motivational internalism. The claim that, necessarily, if an agent makes a moral judgement, then, in normal circumstances, she will possess an appropriate motivation (Section 1.4.2.1).

Normative meaning. The type of meaning necessary to answer practical questions, such as 'What are we to do?' (Section 1.4.2.1).

Relative. A judgement is relative when whether it is correct depends on one among a number of possible frames of reference or contexts (Section 2.3).

Relativism. The view that a set of judgements is relative (Section 2.3).

Report.   To report is to offer a description of a subject. For example, 'I am awake' is a report of my current psychological state (Section 1.3).

Semantic function.   Function that explains meaning (Section 1.4.1).

Subjectivism.   The view that the semantic function of moral judgements is to express beliefs whose correctness conditions are attitudinal, that is, beliefs such that whether or not they are correct necessarily depends on the attitudes of some (actual or possible) people (Section 3.4).

References

Alston, W. 2000. *Illocutionary Acts and Sentence Meaning*. Ithaca, NY: Cornell University Press.

Anscombe, G.E.M. 1957. *Intention*. Oxford: Basil Blackwell.

Ayer, A.J. 1936. *Language, Truth and Logic*. London: Gollancz. (Page references to Penguin 1936/1990 edition.)

Barker, S. 2006. 'Truth and the Expressing in Expressivism' in *Metaethics after Moore*, eds. T. Horgan and M. Timmons. Oxford: Clarendon Press. 299–318.

Björnsson, G. and McPherson T. 2014. 'Moral Attitudes for Non-cognitivists: Solving the Specification Problem' *Mind* 123(489): 1–38.

Blackburn, S. 1984. *Spreading the Word*. Oxford: Clarendon Press.

1993a. 'Circles, Finks, Smells and Biconditionals' in J. Tomberlin, ed., *Philosophical Perspectives, Volume 7: Language and Logic*. Atascadero, CA: Ridgeview. 259–81.

1993b. *Essays in Quasi-Realism*. Oxford: Oxford University Press.

1998. *Ruling Passions*. Oxford: Clarendon Press.

2001. 'Reply.' *Philosophical Books* 42(1): 27–32.

Brink, D. 1989. *Moral Realism and the Foundations of Ethics*. Cambridge: Cambridge University Press.

Brower, B. 1993. 'Dispositional Ethical Realism' *Ethics* 103(2): 221–49.

Camp, E. 2018. 'Metaethical Expressivism' in T. McPherson and D. Plunkett, eds, *The Routledge Handbook of Metaethics*. New York: Routledge. 87–101.

Chrisman, M. 2012. 'On the Meaning of "Ought"' in *Oxford Studies in Metaethics*, vol. 7, ed. R. Shafer-Landau. Oxford: Oxford University Press. 304–32.

Cuneo, T. 2006. 'Saying What We Mean: An Argument against Expressivism' *Oxford Studies in Metaethics* 1: 35–71.

2014. *Speech and Morality*. Oxford: Oxford University Press.

Dancy, J. 1993. *Moral Reasons*. Oxford: Blackwell.

Dreier, J. 1990. 'Internalism and Speaker Relativism' *Ethics* 101(1): 6–26.

2009. 'Relativism (and Expressivism) and the Problem of Disagreement' *Philosophical Perspectives* 23(1): 79–110.

Enoch, D. 2005. 'Why Idealize?' *Ethics* 115(4): 757–87.

2011. *Taking Morality Seriously*. Oxford: Oxford University Press.

Firth, R. 1952. 'Ethical Absolutism and the Ideal Observer' *Philosophy and Phenomenological Research* 12(3): 317–45.

FitzPatrick, W. 2019. 'Open Question Arguments and the Irreducibility of Ethical Normativity' in Sinclair 2019: 138–161.

Gibbard, A. 1990. *Wise Choices, Apt Feelings*. Oxford: Oxford University Press.

2003. *Thinking How to Live*. Cambridge, MA: Harvard University Press.

Harman, G. 1975. 'Moral Relativism Defended' *Philosophical Review* 85(1): 3–22.

Horgan, T. and Timmons, M. 2006. 'Cognitivist Expressivism' in T. Horgan and M. Timmons, eds, *Metaethics After Moore*. Oxford: Oxford University Press. 255–297.

Johnston, M. 1989. 'Dispositional Theories of Value' *Proceedings of the Aristotelian Society*, Supplementary Volume 63: 139–74.

Kirchin, S. 2012. *Metaethics*. Basingstoke: Palgrave Macmillan.

Köhler, S. 2012. 'Expressivism, Subjectivism and Moral Disagreement' *Thought* 1(1): 71–8.

Laurence, S. 1996. 'A Chomskian Alternative to Convention-Based Semantics' *Mind* 105(418): 269–301.

Lenman, J. 2003. 'Disciplined Syntacticism and Moral Expressivism' *Philosophy and Phenomenological Research* 66(1): 32–57.

Lewis, D. 1988. 'Desire As Belief' *Mind* 97(387): 323–32.

1989. 'Dispositional Theories of Value' *Proceedings of the Aristotelian Society*, Supplementary Volume 63: 113–37.

Loeb, D. 2007. 'The Argument from Moral Experience' *Ethical Theory and Moral Practice* 10: 469–84.

Mameli, M. 2013. 'Meat Made us Moral: A Hypothesis on the Nature and Evolution of Moral Judgement' *Biology and Philosophy* 28(6): 903–31.

McDowell, J. 1978. 'Are Moral Requirements Hypothetical Imperatives?' *Proceedings of the Aristotelian Society*, Supplementary Volume 52: 13–29.

1985. 'Values and Secondary Properties' in T. Honderich, ed., *Morality and Objectivity*. London: Routledge and Kegan Paul. 110–29.

Miller, A. 2003. *An Introduction to Contemporary Metaethics*. Cambridge: Polity Press.

Milo, R. 1995. 'Contractarian Constructivism' *Journal of Philosophy* 92(4): 181–204.

Moore, G.E. 1903. *Principia Ethica*. Cambridge: Cambridge University Press.

1912. *Ethics*. London: Oxford University Press.

Ogden, C.K. and Richards, I.A. 1923. *The Meaning of Meaning*. New York: Harcourt, Brace & World.

Olson, J. 2010. 'The Freshman Objection to Expressivism and What to Make of It' *Ratio* 23(1): 87–101.

Papineau, D. 1993. *Philosophical Naturalism*. Oxford: Blackwell.

Plunkett, D., and Sundell, T. 2013. 'Disagreement and the Semantics of Normative and Evaluative Terms' *Philosophers' Imprint* 13(23): 1–37.

Prinz, J. 2006. 'The Emotional Basis of Moral Judgments' *Philosophical Explorations* 9(1): 29–43.

Railton, P. 1986. 'Moral Realism' *Philosophical Review* 95(2): 163–207.

Ridge, M. 2013. 'Disagreement' *Philosophy and Phenomenological Research* 86(1): 41–63.

2014. *Impassioned Belief*. Oxford: Oxford University Press.

Schroeder, M. 2007. *Slaves of the Passions*. Oxford: Oxford University Press.

2008. *Being For: Evaluating the Semantic Program of Expressivism*. Oxford: Oxford University Press.

2010. *Noncognitivism in Ethics*. Abingdon: Routledge.

2014. 'Does Expressivism Have Subjectivist Consequences?' *Philosophical Perspectives* 28(1): 278–90.

Shafer-Landau, R. 2003. *Moral Realism: A Defense*. Oxford: Oxford University Press.

Sinclair, N. 2007. 'Expressivism and the Practicality of Moral Convictions' *Journal of Value Inquiry* 41(2–4): 201–20.

2008. 'Free Thinking for Expressivists' *Philosophical Papers* 37(2): 263–87.

2011. 'Moral Expressivism and Sentential Negation' *Philosophical Studies* 152(3): 385–411.

2012. 'Moral Realism, Face-Values and Presumptions', *Analytic Philosophy* 53(2): 158–79.

ed. 2019. *The Naturalistic Fallacy*. Cambridge: Cambridge University Press.

2021. *Practical Expressivism*. Oxford: Oxford University Press.

Smith, M. 1989. 'Dispositional Theories of Value' *Proceedings of the Aristotelian Society*, Supplementary Volume 63: 89–111.

1994. *The Moral Problem*. Oxford: Blackwell.

Snare, F. 1975. 'The Argument from Motivation' *Mind* 84: 1–9.

Stevenson, C.L. 1944. *Ethics and Language*. New Haven, CT: Yale University Press. 1–9.

1948. 'The Nature of Ethical Disagreement' reprinted in Stevenson 1963.

1963. *Facts and Values*. New Haven, CT: Yale University Press.

Stocker, M. 1979. 'Desiring the Bad: An Essay in Moral Psychology' *Journal of Philosophy* 76: 738–53.

Stojanovic, I. 2018. 'Metaethical Relativism' in T. McPherson and D. Plunkett, eds, *The Routledge Handbook of Metaethics*. Abingdon: Routledge.

Suikkanen, J. 2009. 'The Subjectivist Consequences of Expressivism' *Pacific Philosophical Quarterly* 90(3): 364–87.

Timmons, M. 1999. *Morality Without Foundations*. Oxford: Oxford University Press.

Tormey, A. 1971. *The Concept of Expression*. Princeton: Princeton University Press.

Tresan, J. 2006. 'De Dicto Internalist Cognitivism' *Noûs* 40(1):143–65.

van Roojen, M. 2015. *Metaethics: A Contemporary Introduction*. London: Routledge. 117–137.

    2019. 'Motivation, Recommendation, Non-cognitivism and the Naturalistic Fallacy' in Sinclair 2019.

Warenski, L. 2014. 'Defending Moral Mind-Independence: The Expressivist's Precarious Turn' *Philosophia* 42: 861–9.

Westermarck, E. 1932. *Ethical Relativity*. London: Kegan Paul.

Wiggins, D. 1987. 'A Sensible Subjectivism?' in *Needs, Values, and Truth*. Oxford: Blackwell. 185–215.

Wright, C. 1992. *Truth and Objectivity*. Cambridge, MA: Harvard University Press.

    1988. 'Moral Values, Projection, and Secondary Qualities' *Proceedings of the Aristotelian Society*, Supplementary Volume 63(1): 1–26.

Zangwill, N. 1994. 'Moral Mind-Independence' *Australasian Journal of Philosophy* 72: 205–19.

Acknowledgments

Thanks to Dale E. Miller, Ben Eggleston, and two anonymous referees for their extremely helpful comments on earlier drafts. Continued thanks to Naomi Dobraszczyc for her support.

For Alexandra and Leonora

Cambridge Elements ⁼

Elements in Ethics

Ben Eggleston
University of Kansas
Ben Eggleston is a professor of philosophy at the University of Kansas. He is the editor of John Stuart Mill, *Utilitarianism: With Related Remarks from Mill's Other Writings* (Hackett, 2017) and a co-editor of *Moral Theory and Climate Change: Ethical Perspectives on a Warming Planet* (Routledge, 2020), *The Cambridge Companion to Utilitarianism* (Cambridge, 2014), and *John Stuart Mill and the Art of Life* (Oxford, 2011). He is also the author of numerous articles and book chapters on various topics in ethics.

Dale E. Miller
Old Dominion University, Virginia
Dale E. Miller is a professor of philosophy at Old Dominion University. He is the author of *John Stuart Mill: Moral, Social and Political Thought* (Polity, 2010) and a co-editor of *Moral Theory and Climate Change: Ethical Perspectives on a Warming Planet* (Routledge, 2020), *A Companion to Mill* (Blackwell, 2017), *The Cambridge Companion to Utilitarianism* (Cambridge, 2014), *John Stuart Mill and the Art of Life* (Oxford, 2011), and *Morality, Rules, and Consequences: A Critical Reader* (Edinburgh, 2000). He is also the editor-in-chief of *Utilitas*, and the author of numerous articles and book chapters on various topics in ethics broadly construed.

About the Series
This Elements series provides an extensive overview of major figures, theories, and concepts in the field of ethics. Each entry in the series acquaints students with the main aspects of its topic while articulating the author's distinctive viewpoint in a manner that will interest researchers.

Cambridge Elements ≡

Elements in Ethics

Elements in the Series

Printed in the United States
By Bookmasters